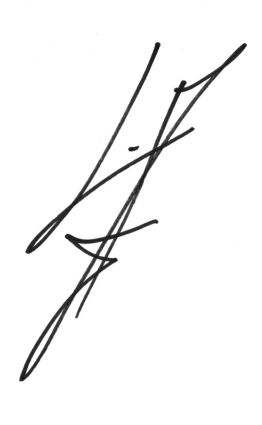

TWICKENHAM

100 YEARS OF RUGBY'S HQ

TWICKENHAM

100 YEARS OF RUGBY'S HQ

BY IAIN SPRAGG

RUGBY
FOOTBALL
UNION

TWICKENHAM
STADIUM

RFU

1909/10   2009/10

CENTENARY
SEASON
TWICKENHAM

CONTENTS

GREAT MATCHES

Running chronologically through the pages of this book, between each chapter, are edited reports of the following 24 great Twickenham matches, described by leading rugby writers of the day.

We are extremely grateful to the newspapers concerned for allowing us to reproduce their material.

Foreword by
MARTIN JOHNSON

LIKE MANY OF YOU WHO ARE READING THIS BOOK I have been fortunate enough to have some very good memories of Twickenham Stadium. The ones I have are just a few of the many hundreds that have taken place in the stadium since 1909/10.

When I made my debut for England against France in 1993 as a late replacement for the injured Wade Dooley I hoped rather than expected that there would be more opportunities to play at Twickenham. I'd watched a lot of games on television and attended a few as a fan and it's a stadium I hold in the same high esteem now as I did when I first visited the ground in the 1980s. It's a special place and not just for fans of English rugby, as I know from speaking to players and coaches from other international sides that the stadium is a special place for them too.

It's easy to fall into clichés like 'iconic' and 'tradition' and Twickenham Stadium has them all but it also provides a great atmosphere and, speaking as an ex-player, there have been many games as a player when the crowd have played a big part in games.

Having had the privilege of playing for England over a ten year period it's never easy to highlight just one or two games that stick out as highlights as every game has key moments in it but if I was really pushed I'd have to say moments like Dan Luger's last minute try to beat the Wallabies, the back to back wins against all three SANZA teams in November 2002 and the home games in the 2003 RBS 6 Nations are right up there with some of my favourite games and hopefully some of yours too!

For Leicester Tigers there are cups and Premiership play-off games to look back on and more recently England games as Team Manager. Each and every game always brings something different but one thing never changes and that is the occasion.

It is always special.

I hope you enjoy the Twickenham Stadium Centenary book and that some of your favourite moments are included inside.

A message from RFU President
JOHN OWEN

IT IS A HUGE PRIVILEGE to be President of the Rugby Football Union during Twickenham Stadium's Centenary.

It took the RFU some time to decide to invest in creating this icon of world rugby - 40 years, in fact, during which 15 different grounds were used for international matches.

Then they asked Mr Billy Williams to find a suitable ground for a national stadium.

Legend has it that it took Billy a year to opt for a local market garden prone to flooding.

A measure of the passage of time is that then many believed the Home of England Rugby could not possibly be located in a place so remote from London and lacking any decent rail link.

Now we are in a London borough and half the 82,000 supporters arrive and leave from seven or eight local rail and tube stations

And I'm sure we would all agree that seldom has a ten and a half acre boggy Cabbage Patch grown such a remarkably fine crop!

This book chronicles Twickenham's history from Cabbage Patch to 365 day a year destination for sport, business and leisure. It makes for very interesting reading.

TWICKENHAM
MILESTONES

Above: The first ever match at Twickenham: Harlequins v Richmond in 1909

SINCE ITS CONSTRUCTION and opening in 1909, Twickenham has been the scene of countless "firsts" and sporting achievements. Here is a whistle-stop tour through time: a selection of milestones in the history of Twickenham as a sporting theatre. The facts may be barely stated... but the milestones resonate with memory and achievement.

1906

In the wake of sell-out Tests against New Zealand and South Africa (played at Crystal Palace which the RFU had to rent at considerable cost) in 1905, RFU committee member William 'Billy' Williams is charged with the search for a permanent home for English rugby to capitalise on the game's burgeoning popularity.

1907

Williams identifies 8.9 acres of market gardens and orchards in Twickenham, south-west London and RFU Treasurer William Cail successfully proposes its purchase for the sum of £5,572 12s and 6d.

1908

Two covered stands on the east and west sides of the pitch, each able to hold 3,000 spectators, are erected. A terrace at the south end of the ground is also built with a 7,000 capacity, as well as a car park for 200 carriages.

1909

Rugby comes to Twickenham for the first time as Harlequins and Richmond cross swords in TW1 on 2nd October. Quins win the landmark game 14-10.

1910

International rugby is staged at Twickenham as England beat Wales by a goal, a penalty and a

England + Wales. January 1910.

try to two tries in front of the sports-loving George V. England wing Fred Chapman earns the distinction of becoming the first man to score a Test match try at the ground after just 75 seconds.

1913

England suffer their first defeat at their new home, losing 9-3 to South Africa in January. Consolation, however, is at hand two months later when the team complete their first ever Championship Grand Slam with a narrow 3-0 victory over Scotland courtesy of a single try from Brisbane-born prop Leonard Graham Brown.

1914

England dispatch Wales (10-9) and Ireland (17-12) at HQ on their way to a second successive Grand Slam.

ENGLAND
V
WALES
1910

The RFU mothball the stadium after the outbreak of the Great War and the pitch is used for grazing horses, cattle and sheep. An instruction to volunteer for active service is issued to the players.

1920

After a six-year hiatus for the First World War, international rugby returns to HQ as England beat France 8-3 in late January.

The Army and Navy descend on the stadium for the first time for their annual inter-services match with the Navy emerging 23-11 winners.

1921

King George V unveils the Twickenham War Memorial.

The first Varsity Match at Twickenham takes place with Oxford claiming victory.

1924

Tries from captain Wavell Wakefield, Howard Catcheside and Edward Myers earn England a 19-0 victory against Scotland and a fifth Grand Slam.

The first omnibus service to Twickenham station is launched.

1925

The 10,500-seat North Stand is opened and HQ attracts a new record crowd of 60,000 to witness the visit of the mighty All Blacks on their 'Invincibles' tour. During the game New

Zealand loose forward Cyril Brownlie earns his place in Twickenham folklore when he becomes the first player to be sent off at the ground (for kicking a player on the ground) as the All Blacks win the game 17-11, bringing to an end England's 12-year unbeaten run at HQ.

1926

England are beaten 17-9 by Scotland in their Five Nations clash in March, their first ever Championship defeat at HQ.

The Middlesex Sevens competition is staged at the ground for the first time to raise money for the local West Middlesex hospital. Harlequins are crowned the inaugural champions.

1927

The first ever BBC radio broadcast live from a sporting event takes place at Twickenham as England play Wales. A map of the Twickenham pitch divided into numbered squares is printed in the *Radio Times* to aid understanding of the commentary, which is where the phrase 'back to square one' originates from.

The new East Stand, with a 5,000 capacity, is unveiled.

1928

The Wallabies play at Twickenham for the first time – only their second match on English soil – but go home empty-handed after an 18-11 defeat.

1929

The iconic Rowland Hill Memorial Gate (now Lion Gate) is unveiled behind the West Stand in honour of the eponymous former President of the RFU.

The RFU agrees to stage the County Championship final at Twickenham for the first time. Middlesex and Lancashire are the two finalists but are locked at 8-8 after 80 minutes and forced to play a replay.

1931

The stadium's legendary wrought iron baths are installed in the home and away changing

rooms, and they are still in use today.

1932

After an investment of £75,025, work on the new West Stand is finished, complete with offices for RFU staff and capacity for 12,000 extra supporters. The South Terrace is also extended, increasing capacity to 20,000.

1935

The Barbarians play London in May in honour of King George V's Silver Jubilee celebrations.

1936

Prince Alexander Obolensky scores a brace of tries in a famous victory over the All Blacks, England's first win against New Zealand at the third time of asking.

1938

Television cameras make their debut at the stadium with live coverage of England's Championship clash with Scotland. The Scots record a 21-16 victory, their first triumph at Twickenham for 12 years.

1940

Rugby is put on hold after the outbreak of World War Two and the stadium becomes a civil defence depot for the next five years. The East Car Park is dug over for allotments while the West Car Park serves as a coal dump.

1946

The Middlesex Sevens and Inter-Services Tournament both return to the ground.

1950

A vast crowd of 75,532 spectators watch England play Wales, a new record for the stadium.

Twickenham railway station is opened.

1953

England's first Five Nations match of the season against Wales becomes the first all-ticket match at Twickenham, with 56,000 in attendance.

1954

The Jehovah's Witnesses stage their first summer convention.

1956

The original Twickenham posts are donated to Rugby School.

1957

Captained by Eric Evans, England beat Scotland 16-3 courtesy of tries from centre William Davies, flanker Reginald Higgins and wing Peter Thompson to complete a seventh Grand Slam.

1959

Above: Sandbags are stored in the East Stand during World War II

1939

The 50th Test match is held at the stadium as England lose 5-0 to Ireland. The match, however,

1945

Rugby returns to the ground for the first time since the start of hostilities as an England XV

RFU Club Competition, effectively becoming the first recognised English club champions. Four years later, the tournament becomes known as the John Player Cup with the arrival of sponsorship.

1974

The world's first ever streaker, Michael O'Brien, a 25-year-old Australian, chooses Twickenham to let it all hang out when he decides to disrobe and race across the pitch during England's game with France.

1979

Planning permission for the proposed new South Stand is granted.

Left: Anti-apartheid protestors stop play in 1969 as South Africa attempt to play London

Below: Twickenham becomes the venue for the world's first ever 'streak'

1965

Cracks appear in the concrete of the South Terrace. Planning permission for a new stand is rejected on the grounds of complaints from local residents, so the RFU begin the prolonged process of purchasing nearby houses to make the project feasible.

1969

The visit of South Africa is severely disrupted by anti-apartheid protests. Nevertheless the tour continues and after five unsuccessful attempts and 63 years after the first meeting between the two sides, England finally manage to beat the mighty Springboks at Twickenham. Tries from second row Peter Larter and hooker John Pullin set up an 11-8 win at HQ.

England wing Timothy Dalton makes history during the Calcutta Cup clash with Scotland – becoming the first ever substitute in a Test match at Twickenham

1971

The RFU celebrates its centenary and Twickenham is presented with the iconic stone lion statue by the Greater London Council. The statue was gold-plated in 1991.

England face a President's XV featuring legends Colin Meads, Brian Lochore and Dawie de Villiers.

1972

Gloucester beat Moseley 17-6 at HQ in the

1980

England narrowly beat Wales 9-8 in February to complete the penultimate instalment of their first Grand Slam in 23 years and popular captain captain Bill Beaumont is chairlifted off the pitch.

1981

The stadium's new South Stand is officially opened by Sir Hector Munro, the Sports Minister and former president of the Scottish RFU.

1982

Erica Roe does her famous streak across the hallowed turf during the half-time interval of England's clash with Australia in January.

Above: Erica Roe proves quite a handful for the Twickenham constabulary in 1982

Right: Will Carling introduces the England team to the Queen before the 1991 World Cup final

1983

England triumph 15-9 over New Zealand courtesy of a Maurice Colclough try and three Dusty Hare penalties and a conversion – their first victory over the All Blacks at HQ since 1936 and Obolensky's heroics.

1984

The RFU introduce the first public tours of the stadium.

1985

Romania become the first international side outside the Five Nations and the Southern Hemisphere 'big three' to play England at Twickenham. The Oaks push the home side close but England finally emerge 22-15 winners thanks to four penalties and two drop goals from Rob Andrew.

1988

'Swing Low, Sweet Chariot' is first sung at HQ as Chris Oti scores a hat-trick of tries on his Twickenham debut against Ireland.

Demolition of the old North Stand begins.

1989

Twickenham becomes an all-seater stadium in the wake of the Hillsborough disaster.

Fiji become the first side from the Pacific Islands to run out at HQ in a 58-23 defeat as Rory Underwood runs in five tries.

1990

Jason Leonard makes his first appearance at Twickenham in an England shirt – the first of an

versus Western Samoa game.

The England versus South Africa clash in mid-November is the first to be played under floodlights at the stadium.

1996

The Museum of Rugby (now known as the World Rugby Museum) opens its doors to the public for the first time.

The advent of professionalism sees England play in sponsored shirts at HQ for the first time as the players run out to face Italy with Cellnet emblazoned on their chests.

Bath take on Wigan in the first ever clash of the rugby codes. Bath uphold union's honour at

incredible 55 caps at the ground.

1991

HRH The Princess Royal visits Twickenham to open the new North Stand and its 14,800 seats.

The Rugby World Cup comes to Twickenham. HQ hosts several matches, including the final, which England agonisingly lose to Australia.

The East Stand is demolished after the World Cup final.

1992

Springbok flanker Christiaan Strauss crosses the whitewash for South Africa and becomes the first player to score a five-point try at

Twickenham. England, however, have the last laugh and run out 33-16 winners.

1993

The new East Stand, with a capacity of 25,000, is completed.

1994

HM The Queen officially opens the new East Stand ahead of the Five Nations clash between England and Wales.

1995

The new West Stand, including new Royal Box, dressing rooms, medical suite and fitness centre, is opened by HRH The Duke of Edinburgh before kick-off of the England

hosts three England Pool B matches, a second round play-off game and both semi-finals – including France's amazing win over New Zealand, one of the greatest rugby matches ever played.

2000

England face Ireland at HQ in the first ever Six Nations game at the stadium following the admission of Italy to the Championship. England mark the occasion with a convincing 50-18 victory, featuring six tries.

Twickenham plays host to its first Heineken Cup final as Northampton and Munster cross swords in front of 68,441 supporters. The Saints edge a dramatic contest 9-8.

The home of rugby union also stages its first ever game of rugby league as England tackle Australia in the opening game of the Rugby League World Cup.

2001

Home supporters witness their side's biggest ever Test match victory at HQ as England demolish Romania 134-0 with Jason Robinson helping himself to four tries and both Ben Cohen and Dan Luger scoring hat-tricks.

Following the decision to introduce an end-of-season play-off format in the Zurich Premiership, Twickenham is the venue for the

Above: England celebrate victory over South Africa in 2002

Twickenham, beating their rugby league rivals 44-19 (although Wigan won the league match 82-6!).

1997

England entertain Australia in the first game of

the Sir Clive Woodward era at HQ. Five penalties from Mike Catt earn the home side a 15-15 draw with the Wallabies.

1999

World Cup rugby returns to HQ as Twickenham

March as a Northern Hemisphere invitational XV take on their Southern Hemisphere counterparts for the IRB Rugby Aid Match. The game is staged to raise money for the United Nations World Food Programme in the wake of the Indian Ocean Tsunami the previous year. The South beat the North 54-19.

Leicester's Lewis Moody becomes the first England player to be sent off at Twickenham in the game against Samoa. The flanker is sent to the stands after a fracas with Tigers' team-mate Alesandro Tuilagi.

The old 'new South Stand' is demolished in a single explosion.

first play-off final. Leicester face Bath in a heavyweight clash in May with the Tigers emerging 22-10 winners.

2002

The term 'Fortress Twickenham' is coined as England go on a run of 18 home matches undefeated, including beating New Zealand, Australia and South Africa on three consecutive autumn weekends.

2003

Twickenham stages its first ever Championship game on a Sunday as England and Italy cross swords.

The England women's team make their bow at HQ against France.

Twickenham becomes an outdoor music venue when the Rolling Stones perform at the stadium in the summer.

The World Cup comes to the home of rugby as the victorious England team parade the newly-won William Webb Ellis trophy before the Varsity Match and again after the match between England and the NZ Barbarians.

2005

Some of the world's greatest players gather in

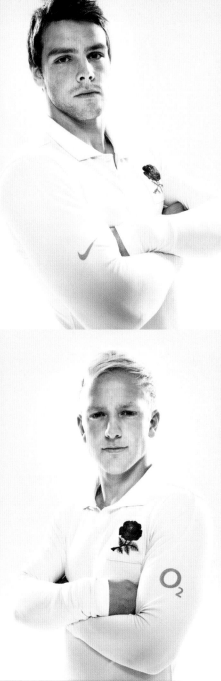

2006

The new 'new South Stand' is opened, bringing overall capacity up to a record 82,000 and making Twickenham the biggest purpose-built rugby stadium in the world.

2008

Lawrence Dallaglio bows out of rugby on an emotional day at Twickenham having played for Wasps against Leicester in the Guinness Premiership final.

2009

The Twickenham Marriott hotel and Virgin Active Classic gym, both part of the new South Stand, open their doors to the public.

The RFU's 'centenary season' celebrations for 100 years of Twickenham begin.

2010

England play Wales at Twickenham in the first Test of the 2010 RBS 6 Nations, just over 100 years after the first ever international at the stadium between the same two teams. To celebrate the occasion England play in a retro-style rugby kit designed by Nike and inspired by that worn by England in 1910 when each red rose would have been hand-embroidered. The rose on the 2010 jersey is a copy of that worn during the England v Wales game of 1910 by Ronnie Poulton-Palmer.

ENGLAND V FRANCE

The Times
Monday, 30th January 1911
By the Staff Reporter

It may have been the afternoon of a smiling April day, and the many French visitors who went to Twickenham on Saturday to see *l'affaire* de football were loud in their praises of the English climate. But the enthusiasm of the male critics who had followed M Communeau's unquenchable smile across the Channel was mitigated by the fact that P Faillot, G Lene and O Vareilles, the three best French three-quarter backs, G Combes, the finest full-back France has ever possessed, and two or three of the French pack as originally compiled were unable to take part.

At the call of 'No side' England had won by five goals, two penalty goals, and two tries to nothing, the margin in their favour being greater than on any previous occasion. During the first-half, however, the French team had almost as much of the game as their opponents.

England's first points came when A. D. Roberts broke away and kicked across to C. H.

Pillman, who gathered the ball when running at full speed and scored an easy try, which was converted by D. Lambert.

The tackling and touch-kicking of the Frenchmen was decidedly good, though their methods of stopping an opponent were occasionally unorthodox, to say the least. When an Englishman was illegally detained he generally displayed a becoming sense of humour.

In the second-half, the English forwards – a fine pack, but slow finding their game – listened to their captain's cry of 'feet' and the French team were overwhelmed.

Evidently the visitors were not acquainted with the method of stopping forward rushes. Practically all the scoring in the second-half was the outcome of excellent forward-play, the English pack often breaking through and going on in a close combined dribble such as gladdens the heart of a Scottish captain.

A. D. Stoop scored the best try of the game when he dodged through the whole of the French side, who were moved to applaud his brilliant bewildering run. Afterwards the game was even for quarter of an hour or so but once more the English forwards took the game in their hands, and the score rose rapidly.

The opposition was too weak to test the ability of the English team. The Harlequins machinery was working visibly, but it seemed to require oiling, the number of missed passes and knocks-on being portentous. Much more coolness and carefulness will be required if it is not to break down against the Irish forwards a fortnight hence.

ALL BLACKS BEAT ENGLAND

The Observer

Sunday, 4th January 1925

By J. C. Squires

By two o'clock the vast slopes of the new Twickenham were covered with people. Around one there were crowds under a shadowy roof, smoking, buzzing, shouting, scrambling over seats; but away at the other end there was piled beneath the sky what looked like a high ridge of pebbles.

In the middle the turf, apparently solid enough to afford a decent footing for something more substantial than Noah's dove, which is reported as having been seen at several places in the Thames Valley. And in the middle of the turf was the band, doing its best.

I saw in an evening paper afterwards that when the English team was being photographed, the band was playing a "melancholy air." In gloomy presage, one supposes a sort of All Black tune. In point of fact it was no 'Chanson Triste' but Elgar's 'Land Of Hope And Glory' which was at least not meant to be melancholy. The teams were photographed and cheered.

The Prince of Wales stepped out and was received with a few bars of the National Anthem instead of his own proper tune. The New Zealanders performed a puppet-show song and dance, whilst the Englishmen, in our well-known casual, insular manner booted two footballs about the ground and then the game began.

The English team missed chances at the beginning which might well have given them a victorious lead. On the other hand, there would have been only a mitigated satisfaction beating a side one of whose best players had been sent off the field just after the start; and in any event the better team obviously won. In one important regard, there was a parallel to the recent University match.

In this game, as in that, the losing side had at least its fair share of the game territorially and more than held its own forward. In this, as in that, the vent was decided by superior combination outside and by an ability to seize chances.

UILDING A LEGEND

LAYING THE FOUNDATIONS

THE STORY OF HOW THE HOME OF ENGLAND RUGBY came to be built in what was a sleepy, rural corner of south west London is as famous as it is erroneous. Twickenham may still be affectionately known as Billy Williams' 'Cabbage Patch', a tribute to the entrepreneurial RFU committee member who found the unlikely patch of land on which the famous stadium rose up, but both Williams and his fabled cabbages are only elements of a more complex tale.

It was on 2nd October 1909 that Twickenham hosted its first ever match when tenants Harlequins faced Richmond. In January the following year, England played Wales in the first international but the seeds of the stadium's inception were actually sown back in 1905 with the arrival of the All Blacks. Even though the game was steadfastly amateur, it was the commercial realism of one particular RFU administrator that was to provide the catalyst for the new ground.

That man was William Cail. A successful and hard-nosed businessman from Tyneside, he had served as the RFU President between 1892 and 1894 and two years later was appointed the Union's Honorary Treasurer.

Sitting in the original RFU offices on the Strand in 1905, Cail surveyed the books. The England game with the New Zealanders had generated a huge amount of public interest but with no ground to call their own, the RFU had hired the arena at Crystal Palace to stage the match at a cost of £3,000. The fixture had yielded a profit of £1,300 but Cail could clearly see

the coffers would have been further swelled if England had not had to pay for the privilege of playing at Crystal Palace.

Wales were already regularly running out at the Arms Park in Cardiff while Ireland had been calling Lansdowne Road home for more than 30 years and Cail realised it was time for England to follow suit, find a permanent home and end the Test side's nomadic existence.

Above: William Cail was the first to understand the need for a new ground

Right: The original minutes from the 1906 committee meeting which set the search for a site in motion

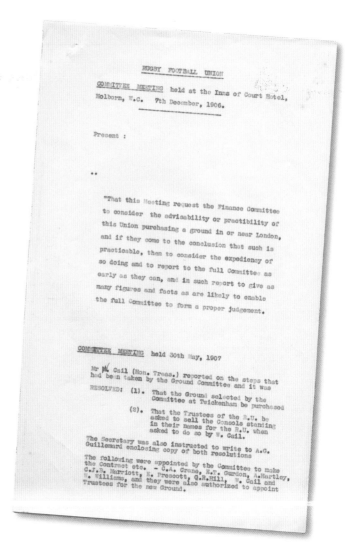

RUGBY FOOTBALL UNION

COMMITTEE MEETING held at the Inns of Court Hotel, Holborn, W.C. 7th December, 1906.

Present :

"That this Meeting request the Finance Committee to consider the advisability or practibility of this Union purchasing a ground in or near London, and if they come to the conclusion that such is practicable, then to consider the expediency of so doing and to report to the full Committee as early as they can, and in such report to give as many figures and facts as are likely to enable the full Committee to form a proper judgement.

COMMITTEE MEETING held 30th May, 1907

Mr W. Cail (Hon. Treas.) reported on the steps that had been taken by the Ground Committee and it was

RESOLVED: (1). That the Ground selected by the Committee at Twickenham be purchased

(2). That the Trustees of the R.U. be asked to sell the Consols standing in their names for the R.U. when asked to do so by W. Cail.

The Secretary was also instructed to write to A.G. Guillemard enclosing copy of both resolutions

The following were appointed by the Committee to make the Contract etc. - C.A. Crane, E.T. Gurdon, A.Hartley, C.J.B. Marriott, E. Prescott, G.H.Hill, W. Cail and W. Williams, and they were also authorized to appoint Trustees for the new Ground.

The view down the Whitton Road to the site where the current stadium stands, pictured during flooding in the early 1900s

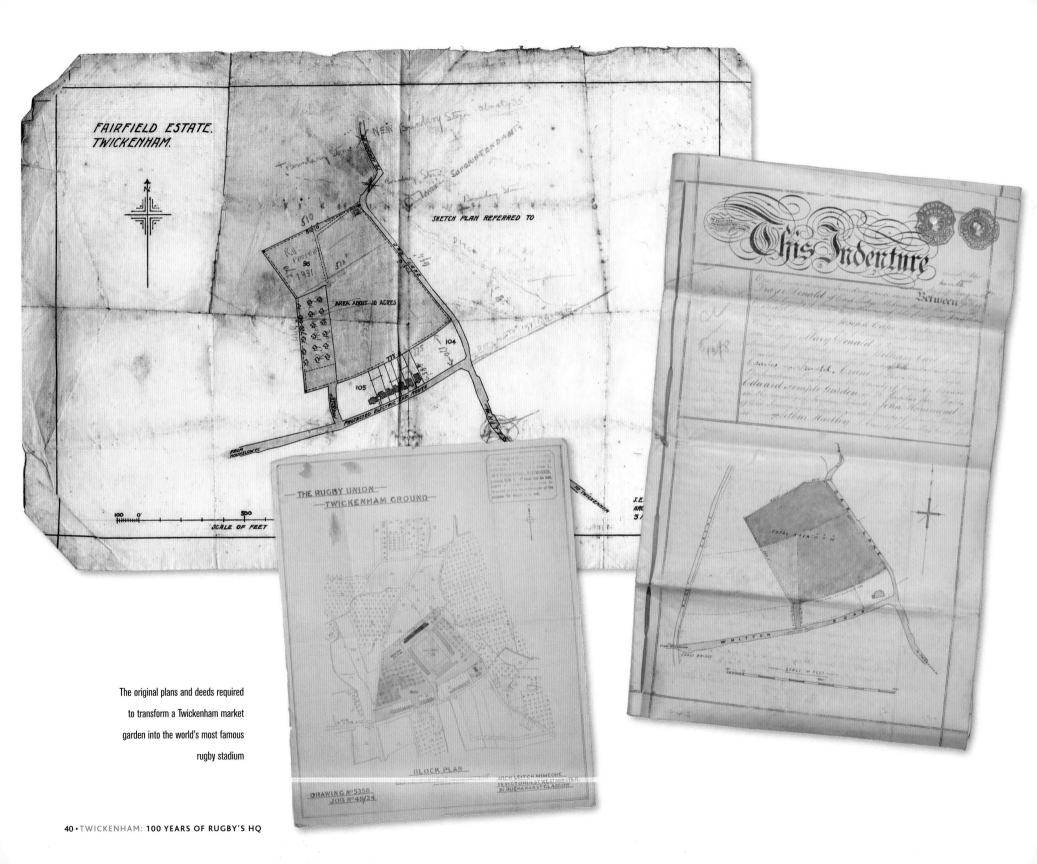

The original plans and deeds required to transform a Twickenham market garden into the world's most famous rugby stadium

BILLY WILLIAMS' CABBAGE PATCH

IN DECEMBER 1906, CAIL confidently put his big idea to RFU President George Rowland Hill. Three months later he submitted a detailed proposal outlining the financial benefits of the scheme and Rowland Hill agreed the plan made sound economic sense. The search for a permanent home for English rugby had begun.

It is at this point in the Twickenham story that Williams enters stage right. Elected to the RFU Committee in 1905, Williams was Cail's choice of chief lieutenant in his grand project and, armed with a modest budget of £7,500, he was charged with finding the land on which a stadium could be built.

Mooted locations in Blackheath and Richmond were both deemed too expensive despite their reputations as traditional and staunch rugby areas and Williams eventually turned his attention to the Twickenham area, where he already lived. The Ivybridge estate was one option but on 1st June 1907, *The Richmond and Twickenham Times* reported that the RFU had purchased an alternative ten and a quarter acre market garden in Twickenham for the sum of £5,572 12s and 6d. The RFU had found its new home.

It was, however, far from a universally popular choice. With the site miles from central London (with one critic cruelly dismissing it as 'fearsomely remote from Piccadilly Circus'), doubts were quickly raised about the lack of transport links and there were also concerns that the blue clay subsoil on the site would make the pitch liable to flooding from the nearby River Crane.

Unperturbed, Cail pressed on and in September 1907 work began in

earnest. One of the first jobs was to clear away the existing fruit trees. Twickenham may be affectionately nicknamed the 'Cabbage Patch' to the legions of fans who have thronged through the turnstiles and gates over the years, but the truth is there were probably more apples and pears than green vegetables in evidence a century ago when the workmen moved in.

The summer of 1908 saw plans for two stands, holding 3,000 fans apiece, at the east and west ends of the pitch and a total capacity of 30,000 submitted to the Twickenham Urban District Council, which were swiftly approved. The building work progressed well, and a widely quoted report that the ship transporting the steel girders for the new stands from Glasgow sank en route south is not actually true.

By October the ground was finally ready and when G V Harvey kicked off for Harlequins against Richmond, a new era for English rugby had begun. The stadium was given a royal seal of approval the following year when England played Wales in January 1910 in front of 18,000 supporters in the presence of HRH King George V and the home side did not disappoint their distinguished guest, running out 11-6 winners. Perhaps more significantly, the game generated gate receipts of £2,000 for the RFU and although the record books cannot testify to it, Cail may well have allowed himself a brief smile of satisfaction as he perused the balance sheet. The building of the ground had stretched the finances but, with the RFU no longer paying rent for an alternative venue, profit margins were up.

Left: Billy Williams, the driving force behind the Twickenham project

BUILDING ON THE SUCCESS

THE OUTBREAK OF THE FIRST WORLD WAR put on hold any plans to further extend the stadium but by the 1920s Twickenham was becoming a victim of its own burgeoning success and, as crowds grew, it was increasingly obvious to the RFU that they needed to increase capacity.

Within the corridors of power there was even talk of relocating. The district council, residents' associations and the Metropolitan Police were all vocally expressing concerns about the lack of adequate transport links but after a feasibility study, Cail concluded the cost would be prohibitive and it was decided to build a North Stand and extend the ground's existing terracing to accommodate 13,000 extra supporters.

The RFU now needed an architect to make their vision a reality and they turned to the renowned architect Archibald Leitch. The Glasgow-born Leitch was already famed for his work on a plethora of football stadia, most notably the Trinity Road Stand at Villa Park, Birmingham, and plans were drawn up for a 10,500-capacity stand.

At this point, Cail's considerable role in the Twickenham story comes to an end. In August 1924 he resigned as treasurer after 28 years in the position and was replaced by former RFU President Ernest Prescott but his departure did not derail the ongoing works. The All Blacks were the guests at Twickenham in January 1925 and although Leitch's new stand was not yet fully complete, a record 60,000 fans were still able to pack the ground to witness New Zealand emerge 17-11 winners.

Right: An early plan of the Twickenham site, complete with graffiti added by an unknown Welshman

Far right: England play New Zealand in 1936. The stadium would remain virtually unchanged until the 1980s

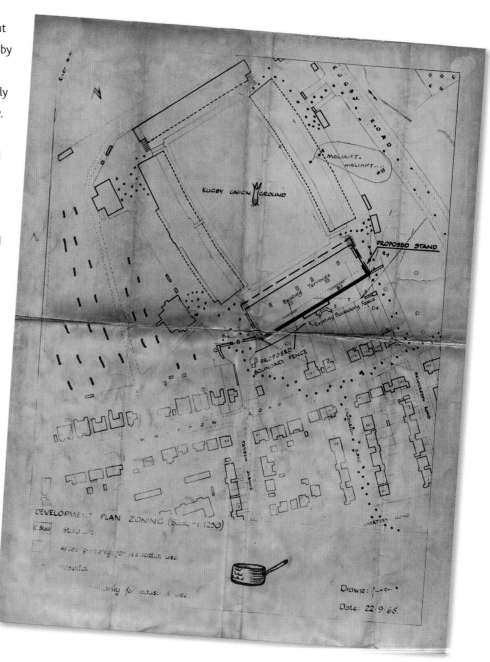

THE NEW WEST STAND

TWO YEARS LATER THE ORIGINAL EAST STAND was 'double-decked' to accommodate 5,000 more bodies but it was not until the end of the decade that the next major phase of development was begun. Two days after the annual Army and Navy match of 1930, work began on tearing down the original West Stand and by 1932 its corrugated, double decker iron clad replacement was in place. In the intervening year, the famous wrought-iron Twickenham baths were installed and can still be found in the current changing rooms to this day.

By now the RFU were firmly committed to regular, money-generating improvements to the ground but any further ambitions were temporarily halted at the end of the decade by the outbreak of the Second World War. Mercifully the stadium escaped any serious damage during the conflict, although a house opposite the West Gate was not so fortunate when it was flattened by a V1 flying bomb, but six years of neglect took its toll. Anti-aircraft fire had damaged the roofs of the stands and when the hostilities ended the West Stand in particular was in a worrying state of disrepair.

The following 35 years in Twickenham's history were to see little substantive change to the stadium. Remedial work on the war-torn stands was undertaken to ensure the ground could continue to operate but otherwise it was a case of cosmetic changes rather than major alterations.

In 1950, new Honorary Treasurer William Ramsay did suggest the Union should consider replacing the original South Terrace with a new stand but his plan was abandoned because the Committee felt the cost of buying the houses and land required to make the project feasible was too high. Instead, the RFU contented itself with installing the iconic Twickenham weathervane, depicting Hermes passing a ball to a youth, in place of the South Terrace clock tower at a cost of £165.

Left: The old West Stand is demolished to make way for the new one in 1932

Right: An aeriel photograph taken in 1935 showing the relatively new North, East and West Stands

NOT SO BEAUTIFUL SOUTH

THE NAGGING PROBLEM of the ailing South Terrace would not, however, go away. The concrete platform beneath it was leaking and although a series of patch-up jobs ensured a degree of stability, it was increasingly obvious something had to be done.

By 1964 the RFU were ready to act and a planning application was made to Twickenham Council for permission to build a South Stand. Unfortunately, the plan was rejected on the grounds the building would be too obtrusive to neighbouring houses and that officials had made no provision for the extra traffic the project would generate on match days.

It was to be a temporary setback. The RFU was acutely aware a South Stand was a necessity and quietly began buying the houses that would be affected by the development with a view to resubmitting a new application.

By 1968 the process was complete but the project suddenly hit a brick wall when the selected building contractors, George Wimpey and Co, put forward an estimate of £620,000 for the work. The RFU had budgeted for a final bill of £400,000 and, unable to stomach the unanticipated extra cost, the proposed South Stand was once again mothballed.

Perhaps thankfully, the Union was distracted from its South Stand dilemma in 1971 when it celebrated its Centenary, a year which saw the addition of the iconic Twickenham Lion to the stadium's landscape. A gift from Sir Desmond Plummer, then Chairman of the Greater London Council, the Coade stone lion had originally been commissioned by the Lion Brewery on the South Bank and had languished in a warehouse for nearly three decades following the brewery's closure in 1947. The Union gratefully mounted the gift on the Rowland Hill Memorial Gate.

The remainder of the 1970s saw further deterioration of the South Terrace and with the introduction of the Safety of Sports Ground Act its capacity was reduced to 15,000 to comply with the resulting health and safety issues. Twickenham's capacity was now down to 70,000 and the late, departed Cail must have been turning in his grave at the prospect of the lost gate revenues.

Above: The South Terrace, conspicuously uncovered and bare for many years.

Far left: A gift from the GLC in 1971, the stone lion statue surveys its new home

THE OLD 'NEW SOUTH STAND'

Right: An artist's impression of the proposed new South Stand

Below: The real thing under construction

Far right: Workers on the new stand celebrate its 'topping out' with an impromptu game of touch rugby

THE CLOCK WAS TICKING FAST on the last undeveloped section of the stadium and by the end of the decade the time had come to resolve the situation as the RFU submitted plans for a new, two-tiered stand featuring 5,500 new seats, 5,700 standing places whilst retaining 1,000 existing seats.

The authorities looked at the £2 million proposal more favourably than they had at its predecessor 15 years earlier and once England, captained by Bill Beaumont, had secured the 1980 Grand Slam – their first since 1957 – the diggers moved in and work began on tearing up the South Terrace in readiness for a new stand.

The design of Twickenham's newest addition was not without controversy. An identical stand had already been erected at Goodwood racecourse and the more vocal and traditional members of the RFU Committee were unconvinced it would be in keeping with the stadium and the spirit of the game.

This time, however, the project would not be thwarted and in February 1981 the shell of the new stand was ready to welcome supporters for the

Calcutta Cup clash between England and Scotland.

Opened by Sir Hector Munro, the Minister for Sport, the South Stand also boasted a banqueting suite called the 'Rose Room' with seating for 400 people. More than three decades after Ramsay had first put forward the idea of consigning the South Terrace to the history books, Twickenham finally had its 'fourth', long-overdue stand.

The two Williams - Cail and Billy - would surely have approved. It had been 76 years since the touring All Blacks of 1905 had exercised Cail's business-orientated mind and led him to conclude that the England team needed its own ground. His vision gave the RFU its home and the game of rugby its finest amphitheatre.

ENGLAND'S GREAT VICTORY

The Times

Monday, 9th January 1928

By Our Rugby Correspondent

England broke a long sequence of defeat or semi-success in matches against teams from the Dominions when she beat New South Wales at Twickenham on Saturday by three goals and one try to one goal and two tries.

Since Joe Warbrick's Maoris made the first invasion in 1888-89, and were well beaten at Blackheath, two representative fifteens from New Zealand, one from South Africa and one from Australia had overcome the picked men of the Rugby Union, and another fifteen from South Africa shared the honours of a drawn game. It may be argued that New South Wales are not Australia, but we are quite prepared to accept the men who had beaten Ireland and Wales and had scored try for try – though without avail – against Scotland as worthy opponents for any country in an international match.

Fortunately, the playing conditions were practically normal and so the Duke of York and the 50,000 spectators had the satisfaction of watching a clash of styles, physique, and temperament that had a fair field and no favour.

The course taken by the game to a large extent supported expectations. The English defence was unable to relax for a single minute but, so long as the forwards more or less held their own in the scrummage, a young, gallant, and enterprising back division were able to do their share both as tacklers and

runners for the goal-line. As, in addition, the pack were able to play up to the best English traditions in the loose, the Australians, for their part, also could not afford to relax or slow down for a single minute. England were quite skilful and fast enough to press home any advantage they might gain in attack, and so it proved.

It is a less grateful task to single out individuals on the English side. K. A. Sellar, at full-back, did not kick so well as Ross, but he was always there while each of the University three-quarter backs was on his mettle and ran and passed and tackled like veterans. Young and Laird played so well together never again to believe that they cannot be kindred spirits. At forward, R. Cove-Smith, as captain of the side, must also be given full credit for a sound leadership.

FIRST VICTORY OVER NEW ZEALAND

The Times
Monday, 6th January 1936
By J. C. Squires

The Prince of Wales was among the 70,000 spectators of a remarkable match, with a still more remarkable result, at Twickenham on Saturday, when for the first time England beat New Zealand at Rugby football. Wales, it is true, had done so in the past, and again only a fortnight ago, but never before had a team of All Blacks been outplayed as well as beaten, and the English score of one dropped goal and three tries to nothing left no doubt as to the relative merits of the sides on this occasion. The New Zealanders themselves at any rate are far too good sportsmen either to question the verdict or to grudge England their belated triumph.

The reasons for the victory were crushingly simple. England had the weight, the developed team work, and they possessed, where it was most wanted, the quality of swiftness too. Happily, the selectors had resisted the temptation to pick a flashily fast pack of forwards, who almost certainly would have been beaten at their own game by a more robust body of New Zealanders.

The first try came after passing was started well inside the English half of the field and, though the ball reached Obolensky too soon, he turned inwards and then outwards at such pace that no-one, including Gilbert, could lay a hand on him. Obolensky eventually grounded the ball behind the posts, but Dunkley's kick fell back when it landed on the cross-bar.

The second came when Cranmer took an unpromising pass, slipped Caughey, and went through. Candler ran up to take a return pass, and Obolensky accepted the next pass and headed for the posts. The way was not clear, however, and Mitchell kept him veering away so far left that Obolensky seemed likely to be forced out of play. Sheer pace, however, told again.

After half-time, Sever was given a clear run and he went on to score in a fairly good position for the place-kick, but Dunkley was not in form in this capacity.

England had actually beaten a Twickenham tradition of their own and English Rugby at large had won the right to claim they had beaten the All Blacks at last.

FORTRESS
TWICKENHAM

STOOP FIELDS THE KICK-OFF.

INSTEAD OF RETURNING HE STARTS UP FIELD AT TOP SPEED.

PASSES TO BIRKETT IN THE NICK OF TIME.

WHO, IN TURN, TRANSFERS TO CHAPMAN AND CHAPMAN DASHES OVER BY THE CORNER FLAG. ALL IN THE FIRST HALF MINUTE.

ENGLAND'S SENSATIONAL START. AN EXAMPLE OF THE GENIUS OF ADRIAN STOOP.

JOHNS, THE VETERAN ENGLISH FORWARD.

COMING ON

COMING OFF

PILLMAN AS A SWOOPING WINGER IS A COMPLETE SUCCESS.

BIRKETT AND SOME WELSHMEN GO HURTLING INTO TOUCH.

GIBBS GETS OVER FOR WALES.

LITTLE GENT IS NOT TO BE DENIED HIS KICK

BANCROFT BOTH AS TACKLER AND TOUCH FINDER PLAYS UP TO THE FAMILY REPUTATION.

F.G.

HISTORIC FIRST WIN

WHEN THE RFU TOOK THE AMBITIOUS, albeit controversial, decision to begin construction of a stadium in the leafy but remote confines of Twickenham more than a century ago, gate receipts and revenues were at the forefront of their minds rather than the creation of the lasting monument to English rugby that it has become.

The physical fixtures and fittings might have changed beyond recognition since the removal of the site's original orchard all those years ago but the inimitable spirit of Twickenham has endured through the seasons and there is no question that the previously nomadic England team found their new home very much to their liking.

The historic victory over Wales in January 1910 not only christened the ground as a Test match venue, it marked the start of its first great, golden era

and for the next 14 years England were to suffer defeat at home just once.

It came against the touring Springboks in January 1913 but, that anomalous result aside, England prospered on both sides of the period of inactivity precipitated by the First World War and claimed the country's first Championship Grand Slam in 1913. Five more followed between 1914 and 1928 and England could irrefutably lay claim to being the kings of Europe.

The 1913 clean sweep came under the captaincy of the late, great forward Norman Wodehouse, while the team's 1914 success was spearheaded by skipper and centre Ronald Poulton and both men became synonymous with Twickenham's burgeoning reputation as a distinctly daunting place for visiting sides to play.

Far left: Artist's impression of England's famous victory over Wales in Twickenham's first ever international

Left: England take on Wales at HQ again in 1914, the home side winning 10-9 this time

England line up before the crucial Grand Slam decider against Scotland in 1928

1930 was another good year for the men in white who recorded this 11-5 win over France at Twickenham

England on their way to their famous and first ever triumph over New Zealand in 1936

Far right: 1935 London Transport poster advocating travelling by tube and bus to see the All Blacks

GRAND SLAMS GALORE

IF THE 1910s WERE A PERIOD OF GROUND-BREAKING success for the England team, the 1920s were a time of phenomenal, unprecedented triumph and in ten glorious years the side recorded four Championship clean sweeps. The first two were masterminded by fly half WJA 'Dave' Davies, who did not allow the small matter of being born in Wales to distract him from his duties, while the innovative leadership of Wavell Wakefield was instrumental in securing the Grand Slam in 1924.

By this time, international matches were beginning to attract huge crowds at Twickenham, putting immense pressure on the local infrastructure. Before the match against the great New Zealand 'Invincibles' of 1925, the huge crowds flocking to the game created an immovable traffic jam stretching down the Chertsey Road and back towards London. The day was saved by King Manuel of Portugal, the owner of a large estate in the area, who allowed cars to drive across his fields and make their way to the stadium cross-country. Despite the chaos, the ground was full and the gates locked a full hour before the 2.30 kick off.

In 1928, in front of another huge crowd, England did the clean sweep again. France, Ireland and Wales had already been dispatched when Scotland arrived in London in March and tries from Jerry Hanley and Colin Laird ensured England were champions once more.

The deluge of trophies ensured Twickenham was now firmly entrenched in the public's affection. England had played 30 Tests at the ground and emerged victorious on 24 occasions and although it was a 29-year wait for the faithful to witness another Grand Slam campaign, it remained a happy hunting ground for the men in white.

Following England's Five Nations title in 1930, the All Blacks tasted defeat against the mother country for the first time at the stadium in 1936 thanks to a certain Prince Alexander Obolensky (see *Great Matches,* page 51 and *Terrific Tries,* page 180) and the following season England claimed the Triple Crown courtesy of the two victories at HQ over Wales and Ireland.

THE CLASS OF '57

Below: England are introduced to the Duke of Edinburgh before the 1957 Grand Slam decider against Scotland

Far right: The England team that went on to perform so heroically against South Africa in 1969

THE GROUND'S NEXT consistently successful phase in terms of silverware came in the 1950s and early 1960s and between March 1952 and March 1963, England lost just four times in 26 outings at Twickenham.

The period yielded two Triple Crowns in 1954 and 1960 but the undisputed highlight was the 1957 Grand Slam. Captained by doughty Sale hooker Eric Evans and with Dickie Jeeps conducting the orchestra from scrum half, England won on the road against the Welsh and Irish to pave the way and when France were beaten at Twickenham in late February, the Championship was within reach.

Scotland still harboured their own lingering hopes of claiming the title on points difference but reassured by the sanctuary of Twickenham's familiar stands and roared on by a vociferous 70,000-strong partisan crowd, England were simply irresistible. Unanswered tries from Phil Davies, Reg Higgins and Peter Thompson comprehensively derailed the Scottish challenge and the home side romped to a 16-3 victory and another Grand Slam. Technically this was the first ever 'Grand Slam' as the phrase was invented by *The Times* to describe England's 1957 achievement.

Dickie Jeeps (England, 1956-62)

"I made my England debut at Twickenham against Wales in 1956. I had played for Northampton against Harlequins at the ground before that but nothing compared to seeing the stadium packed for an international match. It was an incredible sight.

"In my day, club rugby wasn't as popular or as well attended at is today. The crowds were fairly sparse, which meant playing at Twickenham in front of 75,000 people really was the pinnacle of your career. It had always been my dream to play in front of a huge crowd like that and I was extremely nervous before kick-off.

"I had already played for the Lions in South Africa in the summer of 1955 but pulling on an England shirt for the first time at Twickenham was something else.

"The match itself was a mixed bag. We had two great jumpers in David Marques and John Currie but our lineout just didn't function that day and I had some terrible ball to deal with. Any scrum half would have struggled with that kind of service and I wasn't selected for the next game, so the euphoria of playing at Twickenham was quickly replaced by the disappointment of being dropped.

"My favourite memory of the stadium is winning the Grand Slam in 1957 when we beat Scotland. The final score was 16-3 but it was a much tighter game than that. Scotland were a pretty fit side then with some quality players but we played to our strengths in the backs and ran in three tries to none. I've never been a big drinker but I've got to admit I had a few after that game.

"We often talked about turning Twickenham into our palace, making it a place where teams didn't really want to play. We had a good record at Twickenham when I played, so I think we achieved that."

FLUCTUATING FORTUNES

THE ERA AFTER THE TRIPLE CROWN of 1960 was a fallow one. Aside from winning the Championship in 1963, England enjoyed fluctuating fortunes against their Five Nations rivals and the unprecedented sequence of five games they lost at home between March 1971 and January 1973 was a particularly low ebb.

Fran Cotton vies for the ball with Australia's Tony Shaw in 1973

The Twickenham faithful, however, were not totally bereft of the opportunity to celebrate. The touring Springboks of 1969 arrived having never lost at the ground in their four previous visits but England were determined to end an otherwise largely disappointing decade on a high and tries from forwards Peter Larter and John Pullin secured a morale-lifting 11-8 win and a measure of revenge for South Africa's previous impertinence at HQ.

The 1970s may have been a wilderness for English rugby but Twickenham did provide some succour, particularly when the powerful Wallabies twice came calling. The first clash was in November 1973 and England shocked perhaps even their own beleaguered supporters with an explosive performance, three tries and ultimately a thumping 20-3 win.

Early 1976 saw the Australians back in London and again England crossed the Wallaby line three times without reply. A conversion and three penalties from full-back Alastair Hignell merely rubbed salt into the wounds and the visitors were sent home on the back of a 23-6 defeat.

Victory did not initially prove the catalyst for the England renaissance the fans craved but as the decade gave way to the 1980s, their side finally rediscovered their form and self-belief. Second row Bill Beaumont was the man wearing the captain's armband and although pre-Championship expectations were not high, a resounding 24-9 victory over Ireland at Twickenham in their Five Nations opener set a new, optimistic tone.

France were vanquished at the Parc des Princes a fortnight later and when Wales, the defending champions, arrived at HQ in February 1980 on the back of five consecutive wins over England, the stadium held its breath. The Welsh breached England's defence twice but three penalties from Dusty Hare clinched a famous 9-8 win. Beaumont and his troops completed the Grand Slam at Murrayfield a month later and English rugby could hold its head high again.

Bill Beaumont (England, 1975-82)

"I spent my club career with Fylde playing in front of modest crowds, so running out at Twickenham in front of thousands was always a fantastic experience. Some players can get overwhelmed by big crowds but I relished it and the more experienced I became, the more I learned to use the atmosphere to my advantage.

"I can still hear the noise reverberating around the place as we ran out onto the pitch and I can remember looking up at the clock that was fixed on the old East Stand during my debut against Australia in 1976 and seeing 20 minutes had gone already. It felt like we were still in the first minute of the game.

"The more you play at Twickenham, the more comfortable you become. My wife always sat in the same seat, so I'd know where to look and she'd give me a nod or the thumbs up before every game.

"My happiest memory of the stadium would have to be the Wales game in 1980. To be honest, it was probably one of the worst games of international rugby I played in but we just about managed to nick a 9-8 win which set us up for the Scotland game at Murrayfield a month later and the Grand Slam.

"It all nearly went horribly wrong though. Wales scored the second of their two tries with three minutes to go and trailing 8-6, I remember thinking that was the lowest I had ever felt at Twickenham. The Grand Slam was slipping through our fingers but we got lucky when Terry Holmes was penalised for coming in offside and Dusty Hare stepped and stroked a beautiful penalty right between the sticks.

"I was talking to the Welsh lads in the changing rooms after the game when one of the RFU committee came down and said the fans outside were chanting my name. I thought he was pulling my leg but it was true, so I went up to the Royal Box and gave them a wave.

"My last game for England at Twickenham was the Australia match in 1982. Everyone remembers it because of a certain Miss Erica Roe but I remember it because we beat a strong Wallaby side pretty comfortably. I didn't know then it would be my final appearance but looking back, it was a good way to say goodbye."

Bill Beaumont leaps in the lineout against Scotland in 1979

WELL WORTH THE WAIT!

IN TRUTH, ENGLAND'S MOMENTUM petered out somewhat through the remainder of the 1980s but there were two notable games at Twickenham that captured the imagination in different ways.

The first was the 1983 clash with New Zealand. England had not beaten the All Blacks at home since 1936 but Hare was the hero again with a hat-trick of penalties as the Kiwis were seen off 15-9.

The second came in January 1985 and the visit of Romania. In 75 years of blood and thunder in TW1 the only Test teams England had faced were their traditional four Five Nations rivals and the southern hemisphere big three and so it fell to The Oaks to break the mould, paving the way for the impending appearances of sides like Fiji, Argentina, Italy and Canada.

The stage was now set for the 1990s and a period of success that would eventually rival the achievements of Messrs Davies, Wakefield and Cove-Smith in the 1920s.

The seeds were sown during the 1990 Five Nations and although England narrowly missed out on the Grand Slam after an agonising defeat at Murrayfield in the title decider, their performances throughout the campaign hinted at great things to come.

The following season they were not as profligate and with Will Carling proving an increasingly accomplished and influential captain, they completed the Grand Slam with an epic 21-19 triumph over France at Twickenham in March. For the first time in 34 years, England supporters had seen their side wrap up a Championship clean sweep at their spiritual home.

Far left: Rory Underwood is chairlifted from the pitch after victory over France secured the 1991 Grand Slam

Left: Underwood celebrates the final whistle at the end of the same match

HQ MEMORIES

Rob Andrew (England, 1985-97)

"I enjoyed some of the greatest moments of my international career at Twickenham and although it was also the ground where we lost the World Cup final in 1991, I still feel incredibly fortunate to have played so many games at the stadium. By the end of my career, it felt like a second home.

"My first Test at Twickenham was against Romania in 1985, although I've got to admit I have mixed emotions about the match. They kicked off and Will Carling ran the ball from deep. Rory Underwood nearly scored and we ended up with a lineout on the Romanian 22. The forwards won the ball, Richard Harding span it out to me and I dropped a goal on debut after about 45 seconds. That was a special feeling.

"The problem was we played pretty poorly for the rest of the match. Everyone expected us to smash Romania but we only won 22-15 and we were virtually booed off after the final whistle.

"My favourite memory of the ground is probably clinching the Grand Slam against France in 1991. The French outscored us three tries to one but we still beat them 21-19 and the scenes when the referee blew for full-time were incredible. The fans streamed onto the pitch and none of us could get back to the changing rooms. There was just nowhere to go and in the end the supporters chairlifted us off.

"We had missed out on the Grand Slam after getting mugged by Scotland at Murrayfield 12 months earlier and there was this tremendous sense of relief and release that day knowing we had finally done it.

"There's no doubt Twickenham played a huge part in the success the team had in the 1990s. We came together in 1988 when Will was made captain and to clinch three Grand Slams in five years on our own patch was the stuff of dreams. We also beat New Zealand, South Africa and Australia at the ground and we all knew it became a place teams really didn't relish coming to."

CARLING'S CUPS

Bottom left: Brian Moore leads the celebrations after the 1995 win v France

Bottom middle: The Grand Slam champagne flows with Scotland beaten in 1995

Bottom right: Brian Moore after the 24-0 win over Wales in 1992

DESPITE THE AGONY OF LOSING THE WORLD CUP FINAL to Australia in November 1991, the Twickenham faithful would not have to wait long for a repeat performance in the Championship as the 1992 Five Nations became another procession. Carling's side swept all before them and their resounding 24-0 win over the Welsh at home completed back-to-back Grand Slams for the first time since the vintage days of Davies and his all-conquering XV.

Carling was still at the helm in 1995 when England were the dominant force once more. A 31-10 demolition of the French at HQ indicated the side was in fine fettle and it all came down to a winner-takes-all rendezvous with the unbeaten Scots in London. Revenge for the disappointment of 1990 at Murrayfield was duly exacted courtesy of seven penalties and a drop from fly-half Rob Andrew, who contributed 53 of the team's 118 points during the campaign, and England were champions for the third time in five years. Three

further Triple Crowns in successive seasons between 1996 and 1998 only served to underline England's utter supremacy.

If the 1990s belonged to Carling and his team, the early part of the first decade of the 21st century was the era of Sir Clive Woodward and Martin Johnson as England inexorably built towards the World Cup of 2003 and that glorious night in Sydney.

It was during this period that the stadium adopted its 'Fortress Twickenham' moniker and between October 1999 and September 2003, the team claimed a record 22 successive victories at the ground, including the record 134-0 victory over Romania.

England were quite simply untouchable at home and their dominance was epitomised by the immaculate Jonny Wilkinson and during this period the ever-reliable number ten became the highest points scorer in the history of Twickenham.

Will Carling celebrates
his try against Scotland
in 1997

Lawrence Dallaglio and Clive Woodward celebrate victory over South Africa in 1998

England players celebrate the same victory in the Twickenham dressing room

Martin Johnson lifts the Calcutta Cup in 2001

Far right: Joe Worsley scores against Ireland in the 2002 Six Nations

Sir Clive Woodward

"I clearly remember my first game coaching England. We drew 15-15 against Australia and while it wasn't a great game the crowd were excellent throughout and then stepped up a gear when we played New Zealand in the 26-26 draw three weeks later. England led 20-3 at the break and I remember the crowd singing 'We will Rock You' as we walked back into the dressing room. The atmosphere was superb.

"The Five/Six Nations games were always special and the crowd rose to the occasions when we beat Wales 60-26 in 1998 and two years later when we comfortably beat Ireland 50-18 after playing some great rugby in the first half. Great games but perhaps some of my favourite Twickenham memories are from playing the Southern Hemisphere teams when for a period of three years England beat Australia, New Zealand and South Africa regularly.

"From Dan Luger's last-minute try to beat Australia in 2000 to coming back from behind to win by a single point against the Wallabies again two years later and the wins against all three Southern Hemisphere sides in 2002, these were very special times.

"The team were unbeaten at home from the New Zealand 1999 RWC loss all the way through to Ireland in 2004 and this was a tremendous achievement. Along with the 2003 summer tour wins against the Wallabies and the All Blacks these games cumulatively put us in very good shape for the 2003 Rugby World Cup.

"I have special memories of Twickenham and it's an honour to have played and coached there and been supported by a fantastic group of fans."

Jonny Wilkinson scored 21 of England's 31 points against New Zealand to get the ball rolling

THE INVINCIBLES

THE 2002 TRIPLE CROWN was just reward for England's ever-improving efforts but arguably the greatest 15 days in Twickenham's history came in the autumn of the same year when New Zealand, Australia and finally South Africa were the visitors on consecutive weekends.

It had been nine years since England had beaten the Kiwis but a storming performance in front of 75,000 rapturous fans laid that particular ghost to rest and 21 points from Jonny Wilkinson steered his side to a famous 31-28 victory. The Wallabies pushed Johnson's troops even closer a week later but two great tries from wing Ben Cohen and the ever reliable boot of Wilkinson were just enough to secure a 32-31 triumph and complete the second leg of what everyone dared to dream would be a legendary hat-trick over the three southern hemisphere tourists.

The final instalment against the Springboks almost defied belief as England ran riot in a record-breaking seven-try demolition job. Cohen began the devastation and when Lawrence Dallaglio powered his way over in injury time, his converted try took the home side's tally to 53 points while South Africa could muster just one solitary penalty in reply.

Bristling with the confidence instilled by vanquishing the best the southern hemisphere could offer, England went on to claim the RBS 6 Nations Grand Slam in emphatic style in 2003. It began with a win over the French at Twickenham and culminated in a comprehensive defeat of the Irish at Lansdowne Road. It was a record 12th time the men in white had completed the Grand Slam.

Bottom left: Two down, one to go. Australia are buried in the Cook Cup

Bottom right: Hat-trick! Neil Back touches down in the third and final victory against South Africa

FUTURE FORTRESS

THE HIGHLIGHT OF THE CENTENARY season of Billy Williams' erroneously nicknamed 'Cabbage Patch' was always going to be the opening game of the 2010 RBS 6 Nations campaign and the visit of Wales some 100 years after that first ever international at Twickenham between the two great rugby nations.

For their part, the England team has flourished in their century of residency in TW1. The final match of the 2009 Autumn International series against New Zealand was the 255th full Test staged at the ground and in those games, the home side had recorded 162 wins and 23 draws. In the process, they had scored a grand total of 4949 points, including 619 tries and some 489 penalties.

Fond memories indeed and if the next 100 years are anywhere near as dramatic, entertaining and successful, the Twickenham faithful will be richly rewarded.

Microsoft
LAND ROVER
CONFERENCES & EVENTS
TELEPHONE HOTLINE: 0870 143 2400
SPORT ENGLAND
ENGLAND 34 - 0
RFU.COM
DRIVERS JONAS
Costcutter
WHATCAR?
CBRE

Heroic England Snatch Victory

The Observer

Sunday, 2nd February 1958

By H. B. Toft

Two wonderful, individual tries by Phillipps and Jackson, each dazzling flashes of superb artistry, yesterday rescued England, sorely crippled behind and sadly subdued forward, from dull defeat by Australia at Twickenham.

Jackson's try, indeed, was of the sort which would, alone, sustain the faith of England's followers through a score or more of the worst international matches, for it came dramatically not only in the nick of time, a minute from the end of extra time, but as a climax of emotion which Twickenham has rarely experienced.

The score was six-all – Australia having led twice, first by a penalty goal kicked by Lenehan just before half-time, cancelled 10 minutes after the restart by Phillips' remarkable try and then, only six minutes from the end of normal time, and apparently decisively, by a brilliant dropped

goal by Curley. Five minutes later Hetherington equalised again with a penalty goal.

Fortunately, however, Butterfield and Thompson had earned extra time with their injuries. Even this was almost spent when Jackson struck two unforgettable, lightning blows.

Apparently caught in stays and momentarily dithering typically just inside his own half, completely surrounded, Jackson suddenly flashed forward, high on tiptoe and darting and jinking swiftly in turn. The heads of the defenders oscillated dizzily as they tried to place him, but Jackson was faster than any head and in a trance it was a full movement with England's forwards and backs falling perfectly into line from where they had stood at the start.

Thompson, leaning his massive shoulder almost brutally into Donald, was bundled, fighting like a tiger, into touch but England were now on the Australian line. They won the throw-in and the ball was flicked rapidly back to Jackson. The touch was close, two men stood between him and the line, and more were coming fast. Again he checked. Phelps pounced, and as he jumped, Jackson melted like a shadow through him, round Curley, and, with the daintiest of jinks behind the last desperate coverer.

This was not only incredible victory but heroic retribution, delicately and cleanly picked out of disaster and a roar that went up that must have made 50 million Australian sheep turn and look to Woomera.

THE PATTERN-MAKER

Daily Mirror

Monday, 20th March 1967

By Peter Laker

Hail Judd's Juggernaut... the 15-man commando who coldly and scientifically demolished Scottish rugby in an unbelievable six-minute surge at Twickenham on Saturday.

Eleven points were run up against the bewildered Scots in that grand finale – a try apiece by wing Rodd Webb and centre Colin McFadyean; a dropped goal by fly-half John Finlan and a conversion which brought full-back Roger Hosen's tally for the match to twelve points.

For the record, it was England's highest score since 1938 when they totted up 36 points against Ireland and their biggest ever Calcutta Cup victory.

But to 72,000 wildly excited fans, it was much, much more.

It was revival, magnificent and complete, with the final glittering prize the double of Triple Crown and International Championship – Wales willing – at Cardiff on April 15.

How did it happen? The answer lies in the bulldog tenacity of a man who spent most of the afternoon with his busted nose and cauliflower ears buried in the front row at the scrum.

This was the inspiration called Phil Judd, the 31-year-old 14-stone Coventry iron man who took over the captaincy three matches ago after the 23-11 Australian debacle.

In these three matches, we have seen a major sporting miracle worked ironically enough by a

man who runs his own business... as a pattern maker!

What a pattern he has weaved for England!

He has made the pack fight for every ball in every phase and convinced a solid rather than brilliant back division to put their faith in constructive football.

There was no hint of the demolition of the Scots until England went 16-14 in front – the sixth time the lead changed hands in this incredible affair. The all-white forwards were beginning to run the tired Scots into the Twickenham turf with the tigerish back row of Bob Taylor, Dave Rollit and Budge Rogers in the van of every thrust.

The kill came seven minutes from the end. Rollit scooped up the ball from an English heel outside the Scottish '25', broke from the ruck, dummied and sent Rogers away.

On stormed Rogers before slipping the ball outside to Webb – and the Coventry wing weaved through to touch down.

Two minutes later, Finlan deftly intercepted a pass by McCrae and swapped passes with centre Danny Hearn before sending McFadyean over.

DRESSING ROOMS

🌹 ENGLAND	→
DRESSING ROOM 2	→
←	DRESSING ROOM 3
←	DRESSING ROOM 4
DRESSING ROOM 5	→
DRESSING ROOM 6	→
←	FITNESS CENTRE
←	MEDICAL CENTRE
PRESS INTERVIEW	→
MATCH OFFICIALS	→
BALL BOYS	→
DRUG TESTING	→

SCENES

THE CORRIDORS OF POWER

THE FABLED VIEWS OF THE TWICKENHAM PITCH from the stadium's imposing stands are familiar to all of those who have made the pilgrimage to the ground over the years. There is, however, another side of Twickenham which the majority of the crowd never see....

THE COUNCIL ROOM

Twickenham's inner sanctum, The Council Room is the exclusive preserve of RFU council members, past Presidents and their wives on match days and boasts the smallest bar in the stadium. The room features pictures of all of the RFU's former Presidents on panels on the wall. There are 99 photographs in total, although only 98 different faces as Sir William Ramsey appears twice. Elected for the 1954-55 season, he served in the same role again in 1970-71, the RFU's Centenary season, and is the only man to have been President on two separate occasions.

THE PRESIDENT'S SUITE

The President's Suite is a relatively small area with an ante room for drinks and canapés and a dining room accommodating around 40 people, where the current RFU President entertains his guests on matchdays. The President's chair is the tallest in the room and the only one with arms. However, when Royalty or Heads of State are invited, the President gives up his chair.

THE ERIC ROOM

The England Rugby Internationals Club (ERIC) was founded in 1947 by the late Leicester and Headingley scrum-half Bernard Gadney, the man who famously captained England to victory over the All Blacks at HQ in 1936, and ERIC has boasted its own room at Twickenham ever since.

Gadney wanted to form a club that enabled old team-mates to keep in touch once they had hung up their boots and to this day anyone who has

represented England at full Test level is entitled to two complimentary tickets for every international at Twickenham.

Today they convene in their new permanent home, the 237-square metre, 300-capacity ERIC Room in the stadium's West Stand, lined with pictures of some of the 450 who have played for England and a host of other rugby memorabilia.

The entrance hall to the room boasts the famous 'Wall of Signatures' signed by all members and there is also a section for visiting international players who are invited to sample ERIC's hospitality.

Above: The England Rugby Internationals Club

Far left: Twickenham's smallest bar is found in The Council Room

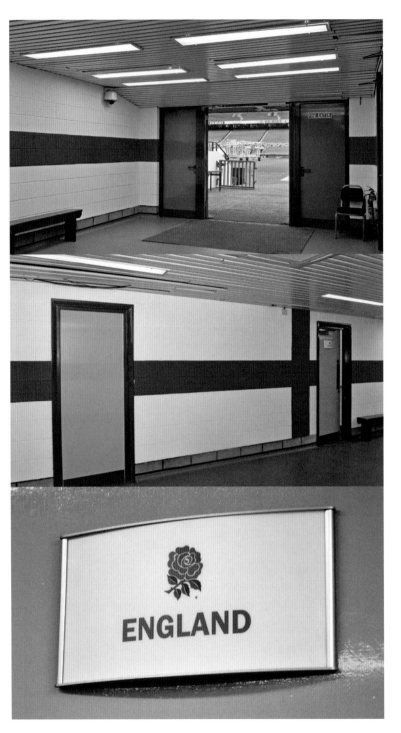

The magical threshold between the tunnel and the pitch

The old (left) and new (right) dressing room doors. Now England always emerge ahead of their opponents

The England dressing room door

Middle right: The coaches' area, just inside the dressing room door

THE INNER SANCTUM

THE FINAL OASIS OF CALM before the players run out to the deafening roar of the Twickenham crowd, the players' tunnel is where the two teams stand shoulder-to-shoulder before kick-off and has undergone a number of subtle changes since the new West Stand was built in 1995.

When Sir Clive Woodward was head coach, the tunnel walls were bedecked with a series of brass plaques that commemorated famous England victories but they were taken down in Brian Ashton's days in charge. The St George's Cross painted along the walls was the idea of former coach Brian Ashton when he took over in December 2006.

Just through the door of the England dressing room is the coaches' room. A large supporting pillar originally dominated this area but it was removed to maximise the available space and as part of this work the England dressing room door was moved slightly up the tunnel so that the home side now emerge before kick-off ahead of the visitors.

The England dressing room just hours before the 2009 autumn international against Australia

The dressing room
ready for action

THE HEART OF HQ

BEFORE A TV-INSPIRED MAKEOVER, the England dressing room in the West Stand was little more than a grey, functional space with a bench and a row of hooks but that all changed when the BBC2 programme *Real Rooms* was invited to redesign it. The new-look facility was unveiled in time for the clash with Wales in February 1998 and the home team immediately took to their new environment, winning the match 60-26.

Today, each England player (the starting XV and substitutes) has an individual booth to change in with a nameplate above their area. The plate stays in place as long as the player remains in the squad and is presented to the player when their England career ends.

RFU Equipment Co-ordinator Dave Tennison is the man responsible for laying out the players' kit before kick-off. Each of the matchday 23 is given two shirts (embroidered with their name, the date and their number of caps), two pairs of shorts and a single pair of socks, all of which they invariably keep as mementos after the final whistle.

One England shirt is hung up while the other is folded and each player

also receives two match programmes, which are placed on the bench.

In the era of Sir Clive Woodward, the dressing room walls were covered with pictures celebrating England's World Cup triumph of 2003 and intended to inspire the team. They were removed, however, when Woodward was succeeded by Andy Robinson in 2004.

Inset: The physios' post-match recovery chart

Left: Jonny Wilkinson's personal space

KEEPING FIT... AND CLEAN

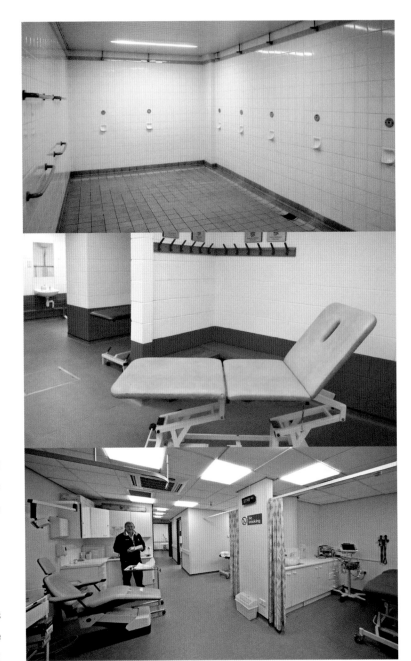

The showers in the England dressing room

A small area in the dressing room used for pre-match massage, strapping etc

The high-tech medical suite, complete with X-ray facilities and dental surgery

Far right: The famous Twickenham baths have been in use since 1931

THE FAMOUS TWICKENHAM BATHS

Although the home and away changing rooms at Twickenham today feature modern, electric showers, the famous original wrought-iron baths are still very much in evidence.

The RFU ordered the baths from The London Allied Iron Founders in 1931. They survived the demolition of the old West Stand in 1994 when the England players were asked to decide their fate and they unanimously voted to retain them.

With six in the England changing room and five in the opposition dressing room, they are now used for the players' mandatory, if not particularly popular, five minute long post-match ice baths. Two of the original baths are also on display in the stadium's World Rugby Museum.

When the West Stand was in the process of being pulled down, legendary England prop Jason Leonard drove to Twickenham in the hope of 'liberating' one of the baths from the room they were being stored in and taking it home. With the help of two demolition workers, Leonard managed to get a bath into his van but was foiled when then Director of Rugby Don Rutherford loomed into view and caught him red-handed.

THE MEDICAL SUITE

The bruising nature of international rugby means Twickenham's medical suite, situated next to the changing rooms in the West Stand, is rarely deserted on match days and the state-of-the art facility ensures those who are wounded in the heat of battle receive the best and swiftest treatment possible.

Featuring treatment tables, a stitching chair for players with cuts and a lead-lined room to house the X-ray machinery hired by the RFU for each game, there is also a dental surgery which is run by Bill Treadwell, who played three Tests for England in the 1960s.

TWICKENHAM'S CELLAR

LOCATED, SOMEWHAT UNUSUALLY, ON THE FIRST FLOOR OF the West Stand the Twickenham Cellar is the stadium's most exclusive dining area and best kept secret. Known as 'Project X' during the ground's reconstruction in the 1990s, the room seats up to 14 people and is extremely well-stocked with vintage wines and port.

Former RFU Secretary Dudley Wood was the man who originally had the idea for the cellar. A discerning wine lover, Wood wanted an area to store the bottles presented to the RFU by opposition teams visiting HQ and instructed the firm of architects commissioned with the West Stand's redevelopment to incorporate an area for this purpose.

A cellar was duly designed but Tony Hallett, the RFU Secretary at the time, thought a mere storage area would be a missed opportunity and suggested

the plans be revised so the room would become a venue for entertaining. Wood agreed and Twickenham got its unique cellar and dining room.

To find out more about booking the Twickenham Cellar for private parties and events, visit the *twickenhamexperience. com* website.

Right: The imposing doors to Twickenham's best kept secret

Inset right: The emblems of England and her rugby rivals are carved in the oak panelling

Right: The Twickenham wine cellar – available for your private party now

INSIDE THE SOUTH STAND

THE AMBITIOUS SOUTH STAND redevelopment delivered by Wolverhampton-based construction company Carillion, was completed in 2006 and marked a significant new era for Twickenham with the inclusion of a hotel, gym and a performing arts centre called the Live Room.

The four-star London Marriott Hotel, complete with 156 rooms, opened in March 2009 and boasts six spectacular, 50 square metre suites with breathtaking views of Twickenham's hallowed turf. The rooms are booked in advance for England matchdays. The hotel also incorporates several bars and the Twenty Two South Chophouse restaurant.

There are also 38 corporate hospitality boxes incorporated within the new South Stand, as well as a series of restaurants including the

800-capacity Rose Suite (part of the Rugby House complex), the Elgar Suite which can cater for 500 and the Churchill Suite, which has 250 seats.

When Twickenham is not hosting a match, the Live Room is a tiered 400-seating venue for live music and conferences. It was officially opened in April 2009 with a performance by 1960s pop icons The Yardbirds and has subsequently featured a 25th birthday celebration for local comedy organisation The Bearcat Club, headlined by Jo Brand. The seats and stage are retractable, allowing the room to double up as both an arts and corporate hospitality venue.

Also incorporated in the stand is the Virgin Active Classic Health Club which boasts state-of-the-art studios as well as steam rooms, sauna, a swimming pool and crèche facilities.

Far left: A room with a view!

Inset: The Twickenham experience in the Rose Suite

Bottom left: The dining area of one of the hotel suites

Bottom middle: The South Stand conference facilites

Bottom right: One of the 38 new corporate boxes in the South Stand

Exit Springboks, triumphant

The Observer

Sunday, 1st February 1970

By Clem Thomas

The sixth Springboks will not shed many tears when they leave for home tomorrow, for they have been afflicted with pressures no other sporting team in history has had to contend with.

There was no let-up at Twickenham yesterday – if anything the demonstrators were more relentlessly hostile than at any time on tour.

Yet the South Africans, after a nervous start, saved their very best performance for what is traditionally the final showpiece of any tour and had the satisfaction of ravaging almost as good a team as the British Isles can produce by three goals, a penalty goal and a dropped goal to four tries.

The Barbarians started as though they were going to humiliate the South Africans and after eight minutes they won a 10-yard

Barbarian Football Club

BARBARIANS
v
SOUTH AFRICA

TWICKENHAM
SATURDAY, 31st JANUARY
1970

Official Programme Two Shillings

scrum against the head for Edwards to scurry around the blind side and feed inside to Arneil, who scored.

Two minutes later, Edwards, who was enjoying a large measure of the ball for the only time in the game and revelling in it, again went to the narrow side and put Duckham away. The wing ran exhilaratingly for a 60-yard try, beating H. O. de Villiers on the way with a twinkling and devastating sidestep.

South Africa came back firmly into the game when Jennings and D. de Villiers came away from broken play and Ellis appeared for the first of so many tries thereafter to score in the corner.

In the second half, the South African forwards were truly magnificent, none more so than Ellis, who looped devastatingly around the field, inflicting enormous damage in attack and yet seeming always on hand in defence. He received huge support from du Preez who, in his 72nd game for the Springboks, broke Gainsford's record number of appearances.

Fittingly, the last South African try of the tour fell

to Ellis when he picked up in the loose and, running with amazing balance for a 16-stone forward, made a monkey of the full back and scored. D. de Villiers again converted unerringly from wide out.

The Barbarians however still had their moments in broken play. After a series of short penalties, Gibson chipped ahead for Duggan to collect on the volley. Spencer looped around him, but put a foot in touch as he went over. It made no difference, for from the ensuing line out Fairbrother dived over.

Bob's a one-man band...

Daily Mirror

Monday, 19th April 1971

By Peter Wilson

The President's Overseas XV beat Bob Hiller by 28 points to 11 at Twickenham.

Can't understand why they will persevere with the feller! It's true he did beat Ireland by his nine points to their six. And yes, he did manage a draw with France, scoring all fourteen points – his own try, which he converted and three penalties.

But look at the Calcutta Cup match. He could score only 12 out of the 15 points registered against Scotland – and they got 16. Not good enough Hiller, not good enough.

And now this. Only all the 11 points, man. It's not sufficient to say you scored the only opportunist try, converted it from the touchline and landed a couple of penalties.

Good lord! You would keep on kicking instead of running the ball, as though you thought that was the only way to win.

Anyone would have imagined you really believed victory would have been achieved when the half-time score of 3-3 proved that was out of the question.

When you, with less than a quarter of the authorised time left, were already a massive two points down.

Why! You'd have to kick another penalty goal then to go ahead. I'm not surprised the keen intellects among the selectors didn't pick you against Wales – and

look what happened then. Wales won 22-6.

In sober truth, Saturday's game, in setting and presentation, had all the trappings of a great occasion.

The Queen, too seldom seen at human rather than equine sporting festivals, had her Royal Marines to play everything from 'Get me to the church on time' to 'Colonel Bogey'.

The trumpeters of the Royal Military Academy Sandhurst blew a special fanfare 'Twickenham' and there was also some Rugby!

Let's examine at least a couple of players who will be carrying the torch for years to come. Law student Bryan Williams, with three tries to his credit, showed that given half a chance he has the speed and resolution to get there.

But, above all, flank forward, Ian Kirkpatrick, yet another farmer, St Francis help those New Zealand sheep! At a little over 16 stone. and slightly more than 6ft 2in it's amazing that he can move at the speed he does.

Yes, a great day full of memories and with the promise of great things to come.

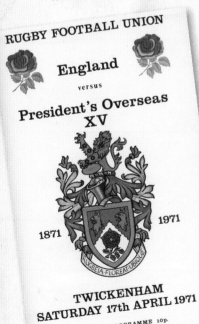

RUGBY FOOTBALL UNION

England

versus

President's Overseas XV

1871   1971

TWICKENHAM
SATURDAY 17th APRIL 1971

OFFICIAL PROGRAMME 10p.

1871   1971

Rugby Football Union

You have been selected to play in

The Centenary Match

England v. The President's Fifteen

at Twickenham on 17th April 1971

Secretary

TWICKENHAM
LEGENDS XV

BILL BEAUMONT

THE 1970s WAS A DARK DECADE for English rugby. The famous five-way tie for the Five Nations in 1973 aside, England supporters were fed largely on a diet of defeat and disappointment and as the seasons passed, the doors of the Twickenham trophy cabinet remained firmly shut.

It seemed an unlikely era in which legends would be born but adversity is so often the catalyst for greatness and so it proved for William Blackledge Beaumont, the man who would finally rouse the England team from its slumber.

First capped against Ireland at Lansdowne Road in 1975, the big Lancastrian second row finished on the winning side just once in his first eight international appearances and although he succeeded Roger Uttley as England captain in 1978, it initially seemed his career would be little more than an unspectacular footnote in the history books.

That, of course, all changed in 1980. England had finished a distant fourth in the 1979 Championship table but under Beaumont's courageous and committed leadership, it was a rejuvenated side that emerged the following season looking to end the drought.

They began with a commanding 24-9 victory over the Irish at Twickenham and then a 17-13

triumph over the French in Paris. The Grand Slam was suddenly, unexpectedly, a possibility and when Wales were beaten in a 9-8 thriller at HQ, England were one game away from the fabled clean sweep. Scotland at Murrayfield stood in Beaumont's path but Fylde RFC's favourite son was not to be denied as England clinched a 30-18 win and the Grand Slam for the first time in 20 years.

In total, Beaumont played at Twickenham 16 times in a career of 34 caps before his premature retirement at the age of 29. The affable lock was unfortunate not to play his international rugby during a period of greater England dominance but his record of six wins and one draw in 11 appearances as captain at HQ, including a famous triumph over the Wallabies, is testament to his inspirational leadership.

An immensely likeable gentle giant, perhaps the enduring Twickenham image of Bill Beaumont is that of the England skipper being chaired off the pitch following the 1980 triumph over Wales, and subsequently receiving the acclaim of the crowd from the Royal Box.

Far left: Bill Beaumont gets into full stride against Scotland at Twickenham in 1979

Right: Beaumont led England to their first Grand Slam in 20 years

WILL CARLING

(ENGLAND, 1988-97)

WHEN GEOFF COOKE controversially handed Will Carling the captain's armband ahead of England's Test with the Wallabies in November 1988, the sceptics whispered that the 22 year old with a mere seven caps to his name would struggle to galvanise a side looking for its first victory over the Wallabies in six barren years.

As the dust settled on his side's 28-19 triumph at Twickenham, the doubts had been comprehensively banished. The youngest player ever to captain England, Carling had spectacularly announced himself on the international stage and in the 58 subsequent games he led the team, an England record, the men in white would enjoy an unprecedented period of success.

A potent physical presence in the midfield, Carling was also deceptively quick and the 12 international tries he scored, seven of which came at HQ, in a nine-year Test match career are testament to his finishing ability and eye for the line.

England were unbeaten at Twickenham in Carling's first eight games as captain but the defining result of his embryonic reign came in the ninth when France arrived in March 1991 for a Grand Slam decider. It had been 11 years since England had completed a Championship clean sweep and although Les Bleus outscored England three tries to one, Carling and his troops held their nerve and their dramatic 21-19 win sparked scenes of wild celebrations at HQ.

The agony of losing the World Cup final to Australia at Twickenham later that year was a chastening experience but the skipper shrugged off the bitter disappointment and, in March 1992, Carling steered the team to a second successive Grand Slam after a thumping 24-0 win over Wales in TW1, scoring one of his side's three tries.

A famous victory over the touring All Blacks in November 1993 enhanced his reputation as one of England's greatest captains and when the team clinched a third Grand Slam following a 24-12 victory over Scotland at Twickenham in 1995, his status as an all-time great was assured.

The Harlequin finished his international career at the end of the 1997 Five Nations campaign in the ranks having handed over the reins to Phil de Glanville but not before leading his team to the semi-finals of the 1995 World Cup and another Triple Crown the following season.

GARETH EDWARDS

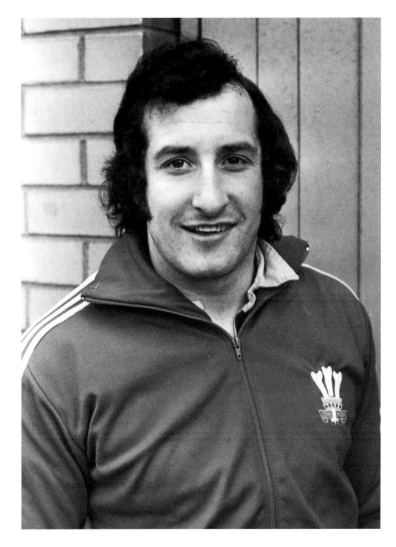

FOR THOSE TOO YOUNG to have witnessed Gareth Owen Edwards in his regal pomp, the reverential tone used to describe him by his contemporaries tells its own story. In the pantheon of the game's true greats, the Cardiff, Wales and Lions scrum half remains in the very upper echelon.

Born in 1947 in Gwaun-Cae-Gurwen, south Wales, he honed his talents at Millfield School in Somerset, a famed breeding ground for rugby talent. Three months short of his 20th birthday, he pulled on the Wales shirt for the first time against France at the Stade Colombes.

The embodiment of the perfect number nine, Edwards had power and pace in equal measure, was a deft and tactically astute kicker and possessed an unerring eye for the try-line. In a golden era for Welsh rugby, he was the undisputed jewel in the Principality's crown.

Edwards was to grace Twickenham six times in a career that spanned 11 years and 53 caps.

His first appearance came in January 1968 and in a tight encounter in front of a capacity crowd, Edwards scored his first international try as Wales battled to a hard-fought 11-11 draw. The home crowd had witnessed the Cardiff magician in full flow for the first time.

A veteran of ten Test appearances for the British & Irish Lions, he was an integral part of the Wales sides that emerged from Twickenham victorious in both 1970 and 1972 but he was to taste defeat in London for the first and only time in his career in 1974 when England held out for a 16-12 victory.

The late 1970s were a period of unrivalled Welsh dominance of the Five Nations and Edwards was at the forefront of their Grand Slam triumphs in 1976 and 1978.

Both all-conquering campaigns began at Twickenham. In 1976 he was on the scoresheet again as Wales outscored England three tries to none in a commanding 21-9 win and two years later, his final bow at the ground, he and fly half Phil Bennett orchestrated a 9-0 triumph that paved the way for another legendary campaign.

Edwards retired at the end of the 1978 season but his place in Twickenham folklore had already long been assured. In 2009 he was voted second in the stadium's 'O2 Player of Century' awards after Martin Johnson.

Inset: Gareth Edwards, voted the second greatest player in Twickenham's history

Far left: Edwards in his heyday inspiring Wales to victory at HQ in 1976

MIKE GIBSON

(IRELAND, 1964-1979)

ELEGANT, INTELLIGENT AND supremely confident in his own sublime skills, Mike Gibson was a true artist of the game and in 15 years of outstanding service for Ireland and the British & Irish Lions his visionary brushstrokes made him a player always worth the price of admission.

Born in Belfast in 1942, Gibson was an outrageously precocious talent who was equally comfortable at fly half, centre or wing and his ability to unlock even the most miserly of defences at the highest level with his intuitive

sense of time and space marked him out as one of the greatest players of his generation.

His first cap came at the age of 21 against England. The Irish selectors named him at fly half for the Twickenham clash in February 1964 and Gibson responded with a beguilingly assured display, showing no nerves as Ireland's back division cut England to shreds in a 18-5 win.

It was the first of eight appearances at the ground for the Irishman and of all the international stadiums he would visit over a decade-and-a-half, it was the one where he

would enjoy greatest success.

His second and third visits both resulted in low-scoring draws. Both games saw Gibson play at 10 but in February 1970 he switched to inside centre and it proved to be a bad omen as Ireland were beaten 9-3.

They were back to winning ways in 1972 but it was two years later that his great hands, sense of adventure and ability to break the line were showcased in all their majesty at Twickenham. Ireland had failed to win either of their two opening Five Nations games but two Gibson tries and two conversions finally inspired the team and they revived their title hopes with a 26-21 victory. They went on to defeat Scotland in their final fixture and Ireland were crowned outright champions for the first time in 23 years.

Gibson's final appearance at HQ was in March 1978. It came on the wing rather than in the Irish midfield and it ended in defeat for the man from Belfast, only his second in eight games at the stadium.

His record-breaking international career finally came to an end in the summer of 1979 after Ireland had twice beaten the Wallabies on a two-Test tour of Australia and it was to prove a fitting climax to a magical stint in Ireland colours.

MARTIN JOHNSON

WHEN MARTIN JOHNSON FIRST stepped out onto the Twickenham turf in January 1993 to face France, the man who was to lift the Webb Ellis Cup for his country in Sydney a decade later was no more than a stop-gap selection, called up at the eleventh hour to deputise for the injured Wade Dooley.

Ten years and 84 caps later, the Leicester second row had established himself as one of the greatest players English rugby had ever produced and in 44 appearances at HQ, he was to enjoy victories over every other major team as Twickenham became a citadel which even the might of the southern hemisphere struggled to storm.

A winner on debut against Les Bleus, Johnson made way for Dooley for the remainder of the Championship that year but by 1994 he was an automatic choice and the following season started all four Five Nations games as England recorded the Grand Slam.

A superb jumper at the front of the lineout and consistently mobile around the park, the lock was named captain by Clive Woodward in 1999 and it was an appointment that proved the catalyst for a golden period for England.

Beaten by the All Blacks at Twickenham in the group stages of the 1999 World Cup, Johnson's side embarked on a glorious 22-match, four-year winning sequence at the stadium which saw England rise to the top of the world rankings and ultimately laid the foundations for their World Cup triumph.

The record-breaking sequence included victories over New Zealand, Australia and South Africa in the autumn of 2002 and Johnson's legacy as his country's greatest and most successful leader was already assured.

His final game at the ground came in September 2003 and although it was merely a warm-up game against France ahead of the impending World Cup campaign, it was fitting that Johnson signed off with a thumping 45-14 win.

In total, 'Johnno' was victorious at HQ 37 times in an England shirt. Twenty of those wins came as skipper and although he earned rugby immortality in Sydney in 2003, it was at Twickenham that England supporters saw him at his indefatigable best.

In 2009, Johnson was voted 'O2 Player of the Century' as part of Twickenham's centenary celebrations.

Inset: Martin Johnson safely delivers the Webb Ellis trophy to the home of rugby in 2003

Far left: Leading from the front as always against South Africa in 2002

JASON LEONARD

FOR 14 GLORIOUS YEARS, Jason Leonard was as permanent a fixture on the Twickenham landscape as the original wrought-iron baths that still proudly stand in the stadium's changing rooms. His phenomenal record of 45 victories in 55 appearances at the ground is one which may never be surpassed.

A veteran of a record 114 England games, Leonard wore the famous white jersey with distinction in Buenos Aires and Cape Town, Wellington and Marseille but Twickenham was always his spiritual home and a place where he was both adored by the home support and respected by the opposition.

His first game at HQ came in 1990 against Argentina and produced the first of those 45 triumphs but it wasn't until four months later that he made a truly indelible mark on the ground as part of the England side that beat France in a 21-19 epic to secure the Championship Grand Slam.

With a chest as wide as the seemingly permanent smile on his face, Leonard was also part of the side agonisingly beaten by Australia

Left: Jason Leonard – 45 Twickenham victories in an England shirt

Right: Running out against Romania in 2001 to become the world's most capped forward

in the World Cup final at Twickenham that year but it was to prove a rare low in the love affair between the player and the stadium. Revenge would come in Sydney 12 years later when Leonard came off the bench to help beat the Wallabies and finally lift the William Webb Ellis Trophy.

The Grand Slams of 1992 and 1995 were both completed at HQ with Leonard to the fore each time but arguably his greatest individual moment at the stadium was in 1996 when he captained his country for the one and only time in his career against Argentina. In a game which England were in grave danger of losing, it was the prop who scored the only try of the match to secure a 20-18 win. These were the only points he ever recorded in Test match rugby.

His final England appearance at Twickenham came in a World Cup warm-up against France in 2003. The crowd did not know then it would be the last time they would see the hugely popular prop on the hallowed turf in a white shirt. If they had, his send-off would have probably taken the roof off.

There was time for one last hurrah, however, when Leonard played against (and beat!) England at Twickenham for the Barbarians in May 2004, exiting the pitch in the 67th minute to a thunderous standing ovation.

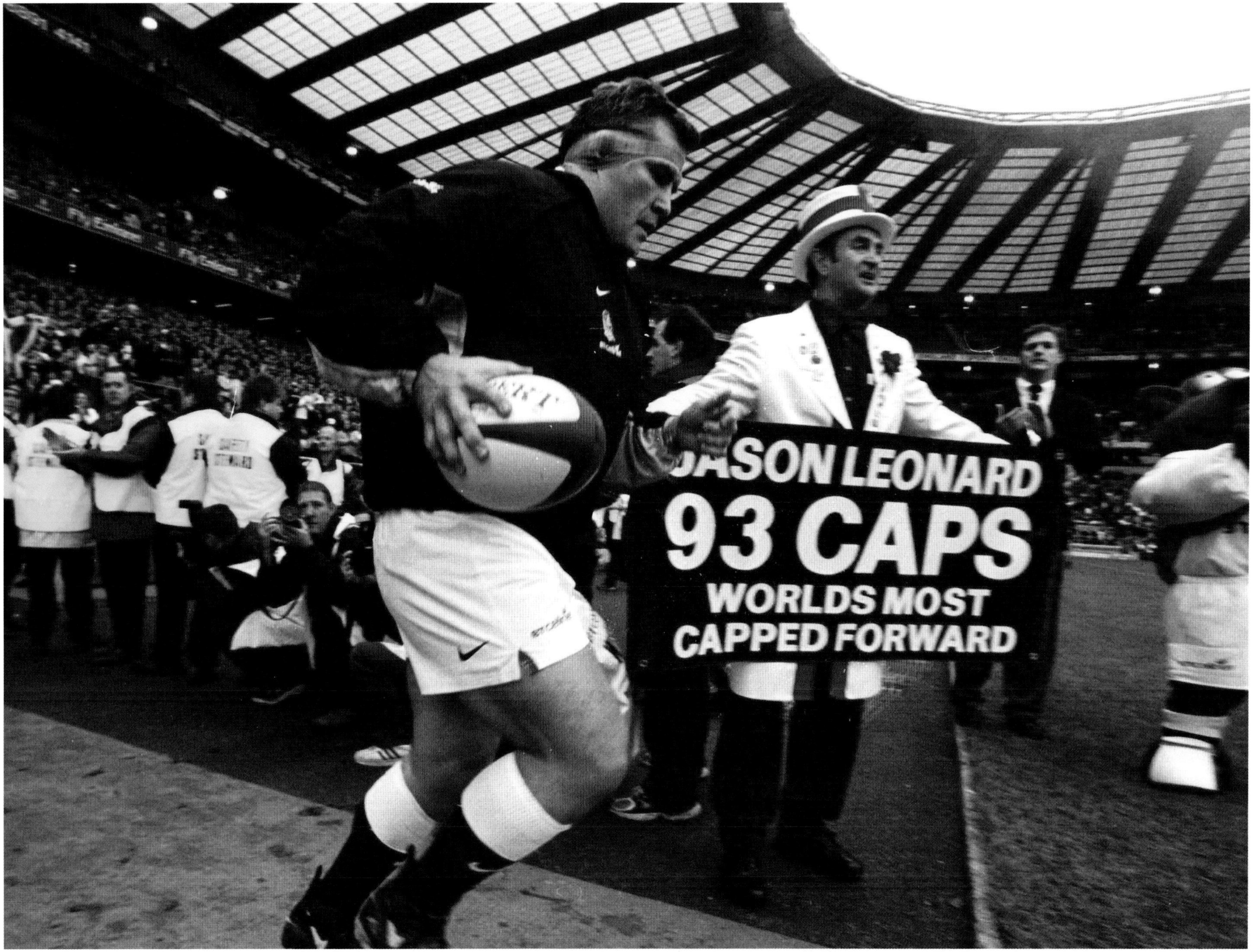
JASON LEONARD
93 CAPS
WORLDS MOST
CAPPED FORWARD

JONAH LOMU

THE SIGHT OF JONAH LOMU stampeding down the wing was frequently enough to unnerve even the most courageous of opponents and Twickenham reverberated to the sound of the giant New Zealander's thunderous charges on four Test occasions as he bulldozed his way to five tries at the ground.

Born in Auckland to Tongan parents, Lomu was first capped by the All Blacks against France in 1994 and his seven tries at the World Cup in South Africa the following year established him as the game's most famous, not to mention feared, player.

His first visit to Twickenham came in 1997. It was an epic contest that ended in a 26-26 draw and although Lomu did not score that day, he was back two years later with New Zealand on World Cup duty, crashing over for his side's second try in a 30-16 victory.

Deceptively quick for such a huge man and perfectly balanced, the six foot five, 18 stone colossus returned to HQ three weeks later for the All Blacks' semi-final showdown with France and although his two tries were ultimately overshadowed by Les Bleus' legendary second-half fightback, it was another dominant individual display that had the 73,000 supporters packed into the stadium purring with delight.

Health problems were to prematurely curtail

his international career after 63 caps and 37 tries but there was enough time for one final Test appearance at Twickenham. The date was November 2002 and the game another epic between the two sides as they shared seven tries between them.

Unsurprisingly, Lomu was one of the scorers. His first try might have been dubious given that video replays appeared to suggest he lost control of the ball as he attempted to touch down but there were no question marks over his second after the restart as the mighty Kiwi burst through Mike Tindall's attempted tackle for a try that typified him at his explosive, irresistible best. Lomu was to play just two more Tests for the All Blacks before he was forced to hang up his size 13 boots but his four muscular outings at HQ will live long in the memory.

Inset: One of Lomu's finest Twickenham performances was for the Barbarians in 2003

Far left: Jonah Lomu performs the Haka before the 2002 encounter with England

WILLIE JOHN MCBRIDE

(IRELAND, 1962-1975)

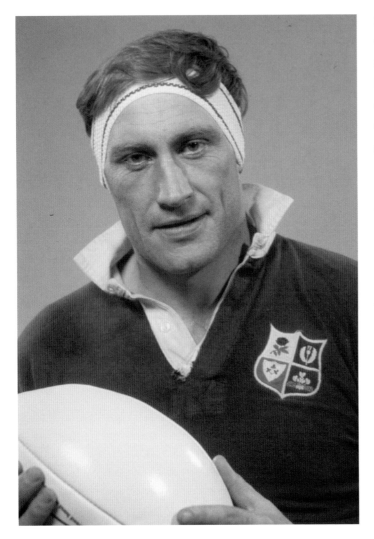

ONE OF THE MOST ICONIC FIGURES in world rugby throughout the 1960s and the early 70s, Willie John McBride was a Jekyll and Hyde character who gave absolutely no quarter on the pitch, whether wearing the green of Ireland or red of the British & Irish Lions, but exuded genial charm off it when the final whistle sounded and the drinks began to flow.

A late starter in rugby terms, the big Irishman did not pick up an oval ball until the age of 17 but he quickly made up for lost time and just four years after being introduced to the game he was running out at Twickenham for his Test match debut in the 1962 Five Nations Championship. The Irish had not won in London for 14 years and although the 21-year-old McBride did not look out of place at HQ, the visitors were beaten again in the English capital.

Four years later, however, it was an altogether different story. By now McBride had the experience of the 1962 Lions tour of South Africa under his belt and nine caps for his country and he and the rest of the Ireland team tore into England at Twickenham. After a brutal forward battle, they emerged 18-5 winners.

Tall, bony and athletic, the man from County Antrim played a record 17 Tests for the Lions on five separate tours, captaining the famous side that beat the Springboks for the first time in 1974, and was named Ireland skipper midway through the 1973 Five Nations campaign.

A member of the Ireland teams that recorded successive draws with England at Twickenham in 1966 and 1968, he tasted defeat at the stadium in 1970 but his final two appearances at the ground both ended in victory for the legendary second row.

The 1972 clash between the two sides was a keenly fought contest that Ireland shaded 16-12 and two years later they outscored the home side four tries to one to wrap up a 26-21 triumph.

His last appearance at HQ was arguably the finest of a Test career that eventually spanned 80 caps and 13 years. By his own admission, Twickenham was his favourite ground aside from Lansdowne Road and in his seven games there, McBride was never less than colossal for Ireland.

PRINCE ALEXANDER OBOLENSKY

(ENGLAND 1936)

IT MAY SEEM STRANGE that an exotically-named refugee should hold such a revered place in the story of Twickenham. After all, Alexander Obolensky played just four games for England, all in the same season, and he was victorious only twice. But then the Prince's legacy is not about mere records or statistics.

Forced to flee his native Russia in 1917 to escape the Revolution, his family settled in London and Obolensky began playing rugby at school. He won two Blues while studying at Oxford University and at the age of 19, and while still a student, the England selectors named him on the right wing for the match against New Zealand at Twickenham.

The date was 4th January 1936. England had lost on both of the previous occasions they had played the mighty All Blacks and 73,000 expectantly filled the ground, dreaming of a famous victory. Significantly, the black and white cameras of Pathé News were also in attendance to capture the game on film.

What followed was the stuff of legend as Obolensky scored two breathtaking first-half tries and New Zealand were beaten 13-0. Twickenham had never seen anything like it.

His first score was all about raw pace, taking the ball from centre Peter Cranmer inside his own half, heading down the right touchline and outstripping the despairing All Black defence.

The second was equally eye-catching. Fly half Peter Candler made the initial break but when the Prince received the ball he was still 30 metres out and faced by a throng of Kiwi players. The New Zealanders may well have expected the England wing to go wide once more but this time he set off on a diagonal burst from right to left. The All Blacks seemed spellbound as he side-stepped past one tackler after another and although New Zealand wing Brushy Mitchell almost got to him, Obolensky was too quick and he was over.

The wonderful black and white Pathé footage of his two tries immortalised a magnificent moment in English rugby history and although Obolensky was tragically killed in 1940 after his RAF fighter crashed on a training exercise, his name remains synonymous with a truly golden day at Twickenham.

Far left: Obolensky in action for 'The Rest' against England in 1938

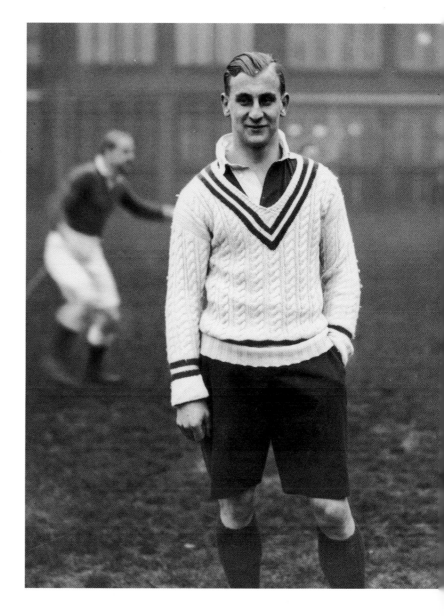

JEAN-PIERRE RIVES (FRANCE, 1975-1984)

Inset: J P Rives, who became a sculptor after hanging up his boots

Far right: the dashing and unconventional Rives at Twickenham

FEARLESS AND FEARSOME in equal measure, Jean-Pierre Rives was a study in perpetual motion on the rugby field and despite lacking the physical stature and power of many of his international contemporaries, his sheer tenacity and courage ensured he will always be remembered as one of the greatest flankers of his generation.

The Twickenham faithful were privileged to see Rives in action five times during a Test career that spanned nine years and he left the famous old stadium a winner on four occasions. It was a record that did not exactly endear him to the home support but even the most passionate Englishman had to concede the blond firebrand was a worthy adversary. A total of 22 of his 59 caps came at the Parc des Princes but his favourite ground outside Paris was undoubtedly Twickenham.

Nicknamed 'Asterix' after the diminutive but indefatigable character in René Goscinny and Albert Uderzo's famous comic book series, Rives arrived at HQ in February 1975 for his first game for France and in a high-scoring contest Les Bleus emerged 27-20 winners.

Two years later they repeated the feat. It was an altogether tighter affair but a try from centre Francois Sangalli was enough to secure a 4-3 victory. It was the second instalment of what was to be a French Grand Slam in which Rives was an ever-present.

His third visit to TW1 was his first as the recently-appointed French captain – a 7-6 defeat – but it was in March 1981 that the iconic flanker enjoyed his finest moment at the ground.

France had already beaten Scotland, Ireland and Wales and as Rives led his team out at Twickenham, Les Bleus were within touching distance of another Grand Slam. England, of course, were loathe to allow their old rivals their moment in the sun in London but with Rives at his combative best and with tries from Pierre Lacans and Laurent Pardo, France completed the prized clean sweep with a 16-12 triumph.

His final appearance at the stadium was in 1983 and the skipper signed off with his fourth victory as France outscored the home side three tries to nil in a 19-15 success. Some England fans were probably thoroughly happy to see the back of him.

After his international retirement Rives resisted the temptation to trade in his boots for a tracksuit and whistle and became a successful sculptor and artist rather than joining the coaching fraternity.

PHILIPPE SELLA

(FRANCE, 1982-1995)

I F EVER THERE WAS A PLAYER to simultaneously confirm and yet subvert the French reputation for producing magical, mercurial centres, it was Philippe Sella. There was no doubt he possessed all the prerequisite vision and flair to prosper in the French midfield, but when he hammered an opponent with one of his bruising tackles it was harder to associate him with the classic French tradition.

In short, Sella was both beauty and beast. An elegant and incisive runner with the ball in hand and boasting superb acceleration, he also visibly relished the physical side of the game and his ferocious, bone-crunching defence was the stuff of legend.

Six of his first seven caps however came on the wing and it was in the number 14 shirt, rather than the number 13 that was soon to become his customary jersey, that he first ran out at Twickenham for Les Bleus in January 1983. He marked the landmark with one of France's three tries that afternoon and English fans had had their first glimpse of one of the game's most durable and explosive stars.

Two years later and now safely ensconced in the French midfield, Sella was back at HQ and part of the side that held England to a 9-9 stalemate. The following year he made history when he became only the fourth player in the

history of the Championship to score a try in each match of the tournament.

In 1987 he scored his second try at HQ as France shaded a tight match 19-15 and although he was to finish on the losing side in his next four cross-Channel trips to London, Sella's contribution to the Twickenham story was far from finished.

The year was 1991 and France arrived at the home of England looking to prevent their old rivals completing the Grand Slam. They were not up to that particular task but by way of consolation they conspired to score the greatest try ever seen at the stadium, running the ball the length of the pitch. Sella, of course, was in the thick of the action, taking a pass from Jean-Baptiste Lafond before offloading to Didier Camberabero, whose lateral kick was collected by Philippe Saint-Andre to run onto and carry the ball over the line for a try of sublime beauty.

Inset: Sella in action at Twickenham for Saracens

Far left: Phillipe Sella was one of the game's most durable and explosive stars

Sella's glorious, record-breaking career finally came to an end in 1995. He had amassed 111 caps and 30 tries for his country and with him marshalling the midfield, France won outright or shared the Five Nations six times.

ADRIAN STOOP

(ENGLAND, 1905-1912)

Inset: Adrian Stoop, taken from an England team photograph in 1907

Far right: Stoop's collection of rugby caps, currently housed at Twickenham's World Rugby Museum

ALTHOUGH IT IS HARLEQUINS' home ground just across the Chertsey Road that now proudly bares his name, Adrian Dura Stoop will forever command a unique place in the long and illustrious history of Twickenham having captained England to victory over Wales in the first international to be staged at the ground.

The son of a Dutch father and half Irish, half Scottish mother, Stoop attended Rugby School and then Oxford University before spurning the advances of Blackheath to join Quins. It was to be the start of a life-long association between the club and player.

His first England cap came in 1905 against Scotland at Richmond. Selected at fly half, Stoop was instrumental in revolutionising the way England deployed their half-backs. Traditional wisdom dictated that the numbers nine and ten were interchangeable depending on which side of the pitch the set piece or breakdown occurred but Stoop rejected this philosophy and argued that both players must specialise. History suggests Welsh and New Zealand rugby had already made the distinction between scrum half and fly half but Stoop was the man credited with effecting the change in England.

The seminal moment of his career arrived on 15th January 1910 when he led England out at their new, permanent home for the first time. There were some 18,000 fans on hand to witness history being made and Stoop's side ensured they marked the occasion in appropriate style with tries from wing Fred Chapman and centre Barney Solomon in their 11-6 triumph.

Stoop only captained his country one more time but he did play at Twickenham on four further occasions and never finished on the losing side. A month after vanquishing the Welsh, England were held to a scoreless draw by Ireland but over the following two seasons, France, Wales and Scotland were all sent packing at HQ.

After his playing days were over Stoop enjoyed a distinguished career as an administrator. He served as Harlequins President for 30 years and also earned a one-year term in the same role at the RFU (always watching matches at Twickenham from high in the North Stand where he could truly study the game). But it was Stoop's part in the historic christening of Twickenham as an international ground for which he will be most fondly remembered.

RORY UNDERWOOD

THE OLD CLICHÉ went that Rory Underwood would fly down the wing at Twickenham as fast as the fighter planes he piloted in his RAF day job. It was, of course, an outrageous if poetically pleasing hyperbole but there was no doubt the elder of England's Underwood brothers was one of the deadliest finishers of his or any other generation.

By modern, Herculean standards Underwood was small but his searing turn of pace ensured he rarely had to sully himself with a physical contest against his opposite number and his tally of 49 tries in 85 games for England remains a record to this day.

For 12 turbo-charged years he dazzled the Twickenham faithful, invariably including his enthusiastic mum amongst their ranks. His debut came in the Championship in February 1984 against Ireland, a game which England narrowly won. He did not score in that game and, almost unbelievably for such a prolific player, his next ten games at HQ all failed to yield a single try. He had no such problems at the Parc des Princes, Lansdowne Road or Sydney's Concord Oval but initially Twickenham proved to be an unhappy hunting ground.

The drought finally came to an end in March 1988. Ireland were the opponents once again but this time Underwood was not to be denied

and his brace of tries in a resounding 35-3 victory saw him come of age on the international stage.

The tries appeared to energise the Leicester wing and his next appearance at the ground in November the same year was equally fruitful as Australia were dispatched 28-19 and Underwood helped himself to another brace.

The floodgates had been well and truly opened and 12 months later he crossed the whitewash five times in England's crushing 58-23 win over the Fijians.

A two-times Lions tourist, Underwood continued to find HQ very much to his liking and he played a central role in the Grand Slam successes of 1991, 1992 and 1995, scoring at the ground against the French in 1991 and Ireland the following year.

His final Twickenham appearance came in 1996, ironically against Ireland once more and although he was unable to say farewell to the stadium with another score, his record of 27 tries in 41 appearances tells it own, compelling story.

Far left: Celebrating the 1995 win over Scotland that secured the Grand Slam

Right: In action against Scotland in 1991

SIR WAVELL WAKEFIELD (ENGLAND, 1920-1927)

The Harlequins and England flanker was nothing if not one of the sport's true visionaries and the way he redefined the role of the back-row forward remains his greatest legacy.

An athletic, abrasive player blessed with natural pace, Wakefield proved flankers could do more than simply contest lineouts and scrums as was the convention. And after playing in the England side that claimed three Grand Slams in the space of just four seasons, it was impossible to argue with his new, dynamic interpretation of the role.

He won his first cap against Wales at Swansea in January 1920. It was a game England lost but defeat was to be a rare experience for the Harlequins flanker over the next seven years and at Twickenham in particular he enjoyed an outstanding record.

His first Test outing at HQ came a fortnight after the loss in the Principality. France were the opposition and a try from fly half Dave Davies paved the way for an 8-3 win.

Wakefield went on to make 13 more appearances for his country at Twickenham, losing just twice, and he was an ever-present in the side that claimed the Grand Slam in both 1921 and 1923.

Appointed captain in 1924, he led England to another clean sweep that same season, scoring one of England's three tries to thrash Scotland 19-0 at Twickenham in March and secure the title once again.

The 1925 Championship saw him switch from flanker to number eight for England and it was to be his position for the rest of his international career, which finally came to an end in 1927 against France at the Stade Colombes.

He continued to play for Quins until 1930 and after hanging up his boots, Wakefield enjoyed a colourful life, serving as a Conservative MP for more than 30 years. He was knighted in 1944 and in 1950 he was elected RFU President. Most of all, however, he will be remembered as one of the greatest all-action flankers Twickenham has ever seen.

WHENEVER A HISTORY OF THE evolution of rugby union is written, the name of William Wavell Wakefield invariably features prominently in the opening chapters.

JONNY WILKINSON

(ENGLAND, 1998-)

ALTHOUGH THE MOST ICONIC image of Jonny Wilkinson's career is of his match-winning drop goal in the World Cup final of 2003 in Sydney's Telstra Stadium, it has been at Twickenham that the England fly half has enjoyed many of his finest moments.

His love affair with the ground began in April 1998. Named on the bench for the Five Nations clash with Ireland, he was pressed into action late on when Mike Catt pulled up with a hamstring injury and at the tender age of 18 years and 314 days, Wilkinson became England's second youngest player after Henri Laird in 1927. It was the first of many milestones he would set at the famous stadium.

Phenomenally accurate with his metronomic left boot, fearless in the tackle and an astute distributor of the ball, the young number ten quickly established himself as a Test regular. He was back in London in 1999 for his first start at Twickenham, against Scotland, and his three conversions and a penalty were to prove pivotal in a narrow 24-21 triumph for England.

Over the next two seasons the points flowed in a deluge for Wilkinson and it was fitting that it was back at Twickenham in the 2001 Six Nations encounter with France that he became England's record points scorer, eclipsing the previous mark of 396 set by his mentor

Rob Andrew.

A succession of injuries were to blight his career in the wake of lifting the Webb Ellis Cup in Australia but he was finally back for an emotional Twickenham return in February 2007, some 1,169 days after his famous drop goal. He marked the occasion with a full house of 27 points, a Calcutta Cup record, as Scotland were put to the sword.

A week later he was back at the stadium with five penalties against Italy which took him past the 1,000-point barrier in Test match rugby. He has since become the game's highest ever points scorer and returned to the England side again in 2009 after another long spell of injuries.

What Wilkinson, let alone England, would have achieved had he not been cruelly robbed of

nearly four seasons by injury is a matter of debate but there is no doubt he will always rank as one of the game's greatest number tens.

Left: Jonny Wilkinson in front of the posts he has conquered so many times

Far left: Wilkinson leaves his Springbok pursuers in his wake in 2000

BARBARIANS 13
NEW ZEALAND 13

Saturday, 30th November 1974

The Guardian

Monday, 2nd December 1974

By David Frost

Respect again for the All Blacks

The All Blacks have gained the respect of world rugby. In scoring a goal and a try and a penalty goal to the Barbarians' try and three penalty goals on a dry afternoon at Twickenham on Saturday they showed that their forwards can now hold in the set scrums the best the British Isles can produce and they gave a grand performance of prolonged attack and imaginative counter-attack.

Some of the most forceful running the All Blacks achieved came in counter-attack and this was an indirect compliment to Carwyn James and the 1971 Lions. Those Lions in New Zealand made a speciality of getting their full-back and wing three-quarters to combine in running the ball out of defence after opponents' kicks. On Saturday, Batty and Williams were repeatedly put into their contrasting strides as a result of the kicks which the Barbarians' half-backs deemed to send straight to them.

Once again the All Blacks owed a great deal to the scheming and probing of Going whose lightning reactions enable him to take advantage of the situation before most people have noticed it exists.

The All Blacks' two scores of the first half came from Barbarians' errors of judgement, so that they led 7-3 at the interval. Two long range penalty goals from Irvine put the Barbarians ahead at 9-7 but then, 12 minutes from the end, Going put up a high kick on the left. Batty tackled Irvine, the All Black forwards drove through and produced the ball and Batty sent across a cleverly judged kick towards the right where Williams, unmarked, gathered and went over for a try which Karam converted.

This looked like the end for the Barbarians, but it was now the dogged character of the 1974 Lions – the character of McBride – came through and led to a rousing finish.

First the Barbarians ignored the chance of three points and preferred to run the ball from a penalty and then, winning it from a lineout on the left, they moved swiftly towards the right, where Irvine, coming up outside Gerald Davies, cross-kicked and Mervyn Davies, following up, got the try which brought the score to 13-13. Irvine could not make the conversion from well out on the right.

Irvine's superlative show lifts proceedings to exalted plane

The Times

Monday, 12th September 1977

By Peter West

In content and result the first meeting of the Lions and Barbarians on Saturday left almost everyone satisfied. The Queen's Jubilee Appeal Fund is now richer as a result of this contribution from rugby football, by £100,000, and its Chairman, Prince Charles, must have thought his journey to Twickenham had been well rewarded.

A greater drive and cohesion at ruck and maul and a superlative performance by Andy Irvine at full back helped build an impregnable lead (23-6) for the Lions, who surely felt they had more to prove in a hard, competitive encounter that smacked not at all of exhibition. But the scratch side, at last acquiring proper coordination in the loose, scored twice in the last quarter and succumbed honourably by a goal, two tries, and three penalty goals to a goal and two tries.

The sun beamed down, the pitch looked lush and manicured as if from a seedsman's catalogue – and Bennett, down the wind, got his Lions off the mark with two early penalty goals, one of them caressed over from 40 yards. It must have seemed like a new dawn for the Welshman, the rain and mud of New Zealand behind him, to stab his foot in firm turf once more and to exhibit that famous side step again.

The contribution of Irivne for the Lions' first try lifted proceedings to an exalted plane. A dazzling piece of acceleration up the right was followed by an inward slant past J.P.R Williams and culminated, as the cover converged, in a difficult overhead pass for Fenwick to score close in, and for Bennett to convert.

In the second period, his intrusion gave timely momentum to an attack that brought a try for Evans, pursuing Fenwick's well placed diagonal kick, and he then popped up again, after a poor pass in the middle, to corkscrew out of a tackle, seize the loose ball and to score himself.

Barbarians began the second period with a characteristic try by Williams, storming through to the posts on a crash-ball from Gravell. The Lions then stretched away but before the finish, Gerald Davies was slipping the tackles and sparking Barbarian counter thrusts out of almost nothing, the blond and always indentifiable Rives was beavering everywhere, and Gravell and McKay ran in the last scores.

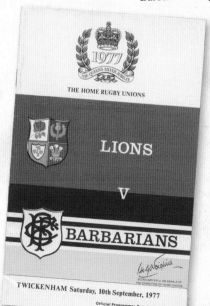

NON-INTERNATIONAL RUGBY

UNIVERSITY CHALLENGE

WHEN THE RFU BEGAN WORK ON TWICKENHAM in 1907, the vision was to create a permanent home for the England team. However, HQ's rich rugby heritage extends way beyond the international game for which it is best known.

Not only was the first ever match at Twickenham a non-international match (Harlequins v Richmond in 1909) but Quins played no fewer than 760 fixtures there between 1909 and 1990 under a unique relationship with the RFU initially forged by the legendary Adrian Stoop. Interestingly, the tenancy agreement between the club and the RFU has never formally expired and Harlequins continue to play occasional 'home' matches at HQ.

Harlequins notwithstanding, the new stadium was first and foremost designed with Test match rugby in mind. England played 11 times at HQ during the first decade of its existence but on 28th February 1920, the RFU embarked on a new era when Twickenham staged the annual Army and Navy match for the first time and in the process opened its doors to a wider rugby fraternity.

The first post-War clash between the services, the game was given a Royal seal of approval by both King George V and Edward, Prince of Wales. And for the first time in the fixture's history the Army selected a non-officer – CW Jones of the Welsh Regiment – in its starting XV. It was the Navy, however, who emerged 23-11 winners but the wind of change had blown the Twickenham turnstiles open and the stadium had ceased to be the exclusive preserve of the England side.

The following year, the students of Oxford and Cambridge descended on HQ for the first Varsity Match at the ground. First staged in 1872, the fixture had variously been staged at The Oval in Kennington and the Rectory Field in Blackheath, before setting up shop at Queen's Club in West Kensington, where it was played for the next 33 years.

The fixture's increasing popularity, however, was causing problems. Queen's Club had a modest capacity of 16,000 and temporary stands had to be erected to accommodate the burgeoning number of supporters. There were also the ground's frequent bouts of fog to contend with – causing the postponement of the matches in 1878 and 1879 – and by 1921 the two universities decided it was time to decamp to Twickenham.

That first match was certainly a star-studded affair. The Cambridge pack boasted three England internationals in the shape of Wavell Wakefield, Geoff Conway and Ron Cove-Smith but it was Oxford who took the honours in a titanic tussle courtesy of two tries from wing James Pitman, the first Old Etonian to win a Blue for the University.

"For a young player, perhaps not so long ago a schoolboy, Twickenham on such an occasion is a formidable sight," wrote Howard Marshall, half of Oxford's second row that day and the author of *Oxford v Cambridge – The History of the University Rugby Match*. "There are the mountainous stands, that great expanse of exquisite turf, the thousands of yelling faces, the reverberating shouts. Though at the time they are only part of a dream from which he is shaken by the shock of a tackle or the strain of a tackle."

Some had feared the move to Twickenham would result in the loss of the intimate atmosphere created by Queen's Club but the two sides' supporters voted with their feet and the 1923 match attracted a record crowd of 30,000. By 1925, 40,000 fans streamed into the stadium to witness the Dark and Light Blues cross swords and the Varsity Match had found a new home.

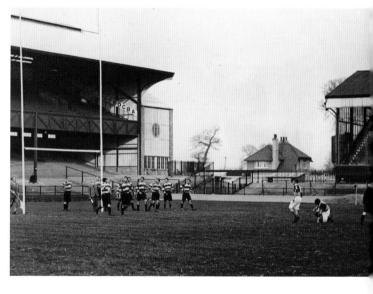

Above: Harlequins in action at HQ in 1926

Far left: King George V meets the players before the first Varsity match at Twickenham in 1921

Right: Rosslyn Park celebrate their Middlesex Sevens triumph in 1954. Note the lack of substitutes!

SEVENS HEAVEN

IN 1926, TWICKENHAM STAGED the inaugural Middlesex Sevens tournament in what was to prove the catalyst for an explosion in the shortened version of the game in England. The Scots had been playing sevens for more than 40 years following the creation of the world famous Melrose Sevens in 1883 but its popularity had remained marginal south of the border.

That all changed when Scotsman Dr Russell Cargill moved to England, joined the Middlesex rugby committee and suggested staging a sevens tournament at HQ not unlike the Melrose event which he remembered with great fondness from his days in the Borders. The RFU considered the proposal and in August 1925 Cargill was given the green light.

Fifty teams entered the inaugural tournament in April the following year as Harlequins, doubtless bolstered by playing in familiar surroundings,

Saturday April 27th 1935 1-40 to 6 p.m.

7 A-SIDE FINALS at TWICKENHAM

Admission 1⁄ Rover Tickets ⁄ Ring Seats 2⁄6 Special Reserved Tickets (Centre Blocks West Stand) 5⁄ (Numbers Strictly Limited)

THE PROCEEDS WILL BE GIVEN TO THE MIDDLESEX HOSPITAL CANCER FUND

defeated St Mary's Hospital in the final.

Twickenham was to quickly become a fixture in the sevens calendar. Harlequins won the event for three successive seasons after their debut win but in 1939 Cardiff finally ended the monopoly of English sides on the trophy. A decade later Heriots triumphantly flew the flag for Scotland and in 1992 Western Samoa became the first team from outside Britain to take the honours. In 1996, rugby league side Wigan Warriors gratefully accepted an invitation to appear at the home of English rugby following the advent of professionalism in union and, rather rudely, proceeded to dispatch all comers.

In August 2001 the decision was taken to switch the Middlesex Sevens from May to August but more than 80 years after Cargill's brainchild was first staged at the stadium, the tournament remains in rude health.

Bottom left: Action from the first ever Middlesex Sevens in 1926

Bottom middle: Western Samoa lift the Sevens trophy in 1992

Bottom right: Martin Offiah of rugby league side Wigan Warriors, Sevens champions in 1996

FOR CLUB AND COUNTY

THE 1920s HAD ALREADY SEEN A RADICAL SHIFT in the type of games Twickenham played host to with the arrival of the Army and Navy and Varsity matches, as well as the Middlesex Sevens, and 1929 witnessed the start of another iconic fixture at the ground that survives to this day.

The County Championship began life back in 1889 but in its earliest incarnation it was a decidedly haphazard affair with a panel of judges from the RFU Committee deciding on the winners. In 1892, regional competitions were introduced to glean four teams to compete in a final round robin competition but by 1896 the more familiar format of a one-off final to crown the champions was adopted.

A final required a suitable venue and up to 1928 the game was staged at a series of different club grounds including Exeter and West Hartlepool, Blackheath and Bradford. In 1929, however, the doors to Twickenham were flung open and the County Championship was given its greatest stage.

The match, in truth, failed to live up to its new setting as Middlesex and Lancashire battled to an uninspiring 8-8 draw but the precedent had been set and the 1984 clash between Gloucestershire and Somerset marked the competition taking up permanent residency at the stadium.

The subsequent quarter of a century at HQ has produced a string of engrossing encounters but none more so than the momentous 1991 encounter between Cornwall and Yorkshire, the greatest final in the tournament's history and to date the only one to have required extra-time to separate the two protagonists.

Some 54,000 supporters – an estimated 40,000 from Cornwall – flowed through the Twickenham gates for the match but after 54 minutes it was the Yorkshire contingent in the ground who were cheering as their side took a seemingly unassailable 16-3 lead.

Cornwall, however, had other ideas and in what was to prove one of the most epic comebacks in Twickenham's long and illustrious history, Chris Alcock's side rallied and when scrum half Richard Nancekivell darted over in the dying seconds of normal time the scores were level at 16-16.

The potentially match-winning conversion went agonisingly wide of the right-hand post but the momentum was now with Cornwall and veteran wing Tommy Bassett and fly half Billy Peters both breached the Yorkshire defence in extra-time to set up a famous 29-20 triumph. Twickenham echoed to the sound of 'Trelawny', the Cornish national anthem, as Alcock climbed the steps to receive the trophy from the Duke of Edinburgh and Cornwall were the champions for the first time since 1908.

"The greatest comeback in the history of Cornish rugby sent Duchy fans delirious with delighted disbelief at the end of Saturday's tumultuous triumph at Twickenham," reported the unashamedly partisan *Cornishman* newspaper on its front page. "As the final whistle blew, signalling an unforgettable 29-20 victory over the White Rose of Yorkshire, the realisation suddenly dawned that Cornwall had bridged an 83-year gap and become county champions for the second time. A sea of black-and-gold bedecked supporters instantly invaded Twickenham's hallowed turf as Trelawny's Army raced to hail their conquering heroes. The rapturous roar that greeted the players as the coveted prize was held aloft could probably have been heard in neighbouring Richmond."

Above: Action from the famous Cornwall v Yorkshire match of 1991

Far left: Cornwall invades HQ again eight years later

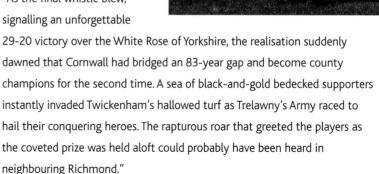

IT'S A KNOCKOUT

THE NEXT MAJOR ADDITION to Twickenham's burgeoning list of non-international fixtures was the advent of English rugby's first national knockout cup competition in 1972. Originally and somewhat prosaically known as the RFU Club Competition before it was rebranded the John Player Cup four years later, it has also been called the Pilkington Glass, Tetley's Bitter and Powergen Cup over the subsequent years and in its current format as an Anglo-Welsh club competition, it has been re-named the EDF Energy Cup.

The inaugural 1972 clash between Gloucester and Moseley was a bad tempered affair and England second row Nigel Horton earned himself an early dip in Twickenham's famous wrought iron baths after a none-too-subtle punch at Gloucester's Dick Smith. The dismissal and injuries meant Moseley finished the game with just 12 men and the Cherry and Whites closed out a 17-6 victory.

All the subsequent finals have been staged at HQ, arguably the finest coming in 2004 when Newcastle and Sale conjured up a 70-point thriller in front of a 48,590 crowd that was only settled in the final minutes.

The deluge of points began as early as the seventh minute when Falcons flanker Warren Britz crashed over. It was the first of seven tries on the day but the pivotal score came, in oddly symmetrical fashion, seven minutes from time when Newcastle back rower Phil Dowson muscled his way across the try line to seal a 37-33 victory.

"The great entertainers are back," reported Newcastle newspaper *The Sunday Sun*. "The Falcons came from behind to win a fantastic Powergen Cup Final in the dying minutes. Just as they did three years ago, Newcastle looked down and out at 33-30 with seven minutes left but somehow managed to come up with a great try from England Sevens hero Dowson to win the game and send their 25,000 fans home ecstatic.

"And they did it with style, with panache and by sticking to their running rugby creed. 'The Blaydon Races' rang out round Twickenham as the players enjoyed a lap of honour led by skipper Hugh Vyvyan, as shattered Sale could only watch from the centre spot."

Right: A Leicester tiger on the prowl during the John Player Cup final of 1983

Far right: Cardiff Blues celebrate their 2009 EDF Energy Cup final win

Newcastle Falcons'
Joe Shaw soars over the
line to score in the epic
2004 final against Sale

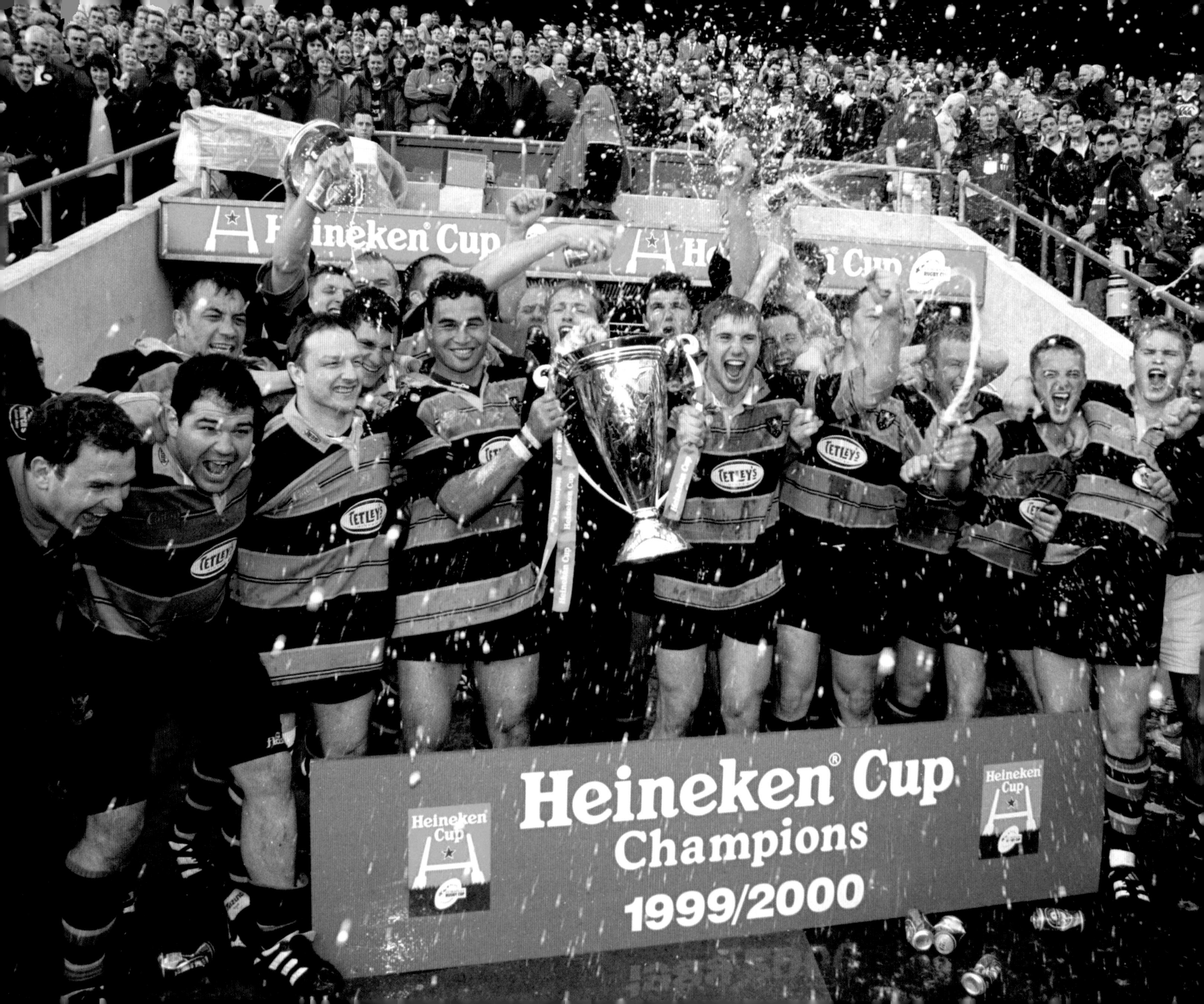

Heineken Cup
Champions
1999/2000

EUROPEAN UNION

THE NEW MILLENNIUM SAW TWICKENHAM welcome two more high-profile fixtures to the ground in quick succession. The first was the Heineken Cup final in 2000 and 12 months later HQ was the venue for the ground-breaking Premiership play-off final.

The Heineken Cup was in its fifth season when it finally came to the stadium. The Cardiff Arms Park (twice), the Stade Lescure in Bordeaux and Lansdowne Road had hosted the previous finals but in 2000 Twickenham was chosen to host the eagerly-anticipated battle to be crowned club champions of Europe and a crowd of over 68,000 poured into the ground to witness the Anglo-Irish showdown between Northampton and Munster.

Thunder, lightning and torrential rain on the morning of the match mercifully gave way to brilliant sunshine by kick-off and although the contest lacked a certain finesse and flair, it was unsurpassed in terms of drama and tension.

Munster scored the game's only try through Ireland flanker David Wallace but the nerveless kicking of Saints full back Paul Grayson was the difference between the two sides. Grayson landed three penalties while Ronan O'Gara missed a last-minute penalty for the Irish province and when the final whistle sounded, Northampton were 9-8 victors and the proud holders of the first major trophy in the club's 120-year history.

"The scenes at the end beggared belief," wrote Paul Ackford the following day in *The Sunday Telegraph*. "Supporters and replacements piled on to the field after the final whistle to join both teams standing defiantly in separate circles in the middle of the pitch. Northampton linked arms and cavorted in boundless joy and enthusiasm while Munster bowed their heads in silent contemplation.

"There were nearly 70,000 people at Twickenham to watch the two sides slug it out. The rivalry between the supporters was as captivating, intense and good-humoured as that between the players and Twickenham, almost as an act of defiance, showed that it can work as a sporting arena. If rugby can continue to find days like this at club level then it surely has a future, and a bright one at that."

The stadium has staged two subsequent Heineken Cup finals and, perhaps fittingly, the Home of England Rugby has proved to be something of a lucky charm for English clubs. Northampton's triumph was followed by Wasps' 27-20 victory over Toulouse in 2004 and three years later the London side made it a hat-trick of Twickenham triumphs for Premiership sides with their 25-9 win over Leicester.

Far left: Northampton celebrate their Heineken Cup win in 2000

Below: Leicester's Daryl Gibson in the 2007 Heineken Cup final against Wasps

A small crowd, but a massive moment for Gloucester, lifting the 2002 Zurich Championship trophy

Leicester's Deacon brothers parade the Guinness Premiership trophy in 2007

Twickenham must feel like home to Wasps fans after winning nine finals in nine years since 1999

Far right: Wasps' Raphael Ibanez emerges from a pile of bodies like a Roman gladiator during the Guinness Premiership final of 2008

PLAY-OFFS AT HQ

THE ADVENT OF THE PREMIERSHIP PLAY-OFF FINAL in 2001 was a watershed for league rugby in England but the concept initially failed to capture the public imagination and a modest crowd of 33,500 were at Twickenham that first year to see Leicester beat Bath 22-10.

Only 28,500 were at the ground the following year for Gloucester's narrow win over Bristol but 2003 saw the rugby fraternity finally and overwhelmingly embrace the new format. Wasps faced Gloucester on a searingly hot day and some 42,000 arrived at HQ for the showpiece game as the Londoners crushed the Cherry and Whites, the first of three successive victories in the fixture.

Since then, the play-off final has gone from strength to strength and the 2008 clash between Wasps and Leicester drew a world record crowd for a club game of 82,000 and was a thoroughly emotional occasion that marked the end of Lawrence Dallaglio's playing career.

Wasps stormed clear through touchdowns by flanker Tom Rees and wing Josh Lewsey, while full back Mark van Gisbergen weighed in with five successful kicks. And although the Tigers finally roused themselves in the second-half to ensure the Londoners were unable to relax, Dallaglio duly signed off with yet another victory in a major final.

"They craved a fairy tale and they were granted their hearts' desire," ran *The Independent* report on the match. "Thousands upon thousands of Wasps supporters – most of whom had not previously realised they were anything of the sort, judging by the average gate at England's most successful club – watched Lawrence Dallaglio, rugby's favourite West End wide boy, end his career with the Guinness Premiership trophy before a record crowd of almost 82,000."

And Wasps fans are now assured of at least one visit a year to HQ having reached an agreement with the RFU to stage an annual fixture at Twickenham to celebrate St George's Day.

The Observer
Sunday, 20th November 1983
By Clem Thomas

The arrival of Captain Marvellous

It might not have been one of the most fluent internationals one has seen but for raw vigour, courage and high excitement it was something to marvel at as England, through the superb physical commitment of their forwards, emulated their predecessors of 1936 and 1973 to gain only their third win over the All Blacks in 13 matches by a goal and three penalty goals to a goal and a penalty goal.

It was a triumph and a personal vindication for Peter Wheeler, who has had to wait until a week before his 35th birthday to justify his claim to be England captain. He led by example and provoked one of the best performances from an England pack for many a long day.

If you had to single out where the England forwards were at their most commanding, it was in the loose, where Winterbottom, Scott and Simpson eclipsed the principal New Zealand forward strength of Shaw, Mexted and Hobbs. Victory must have been a sweet moment for Hare, Woodward, Carleton, Colclough, Bainbridge and Winterbottom after their tribulations [with the Lions] during the summer.

Apart from the tempestuous performance of the England pack, every one of whom gave his all, we saw some decisive running by Youngs and a solid defensive performance by the England three-quarters, who for the most part were supernumeraries to the kicking strategy. Had Hare, who missed four penalties, been in better form with the boot, England would have won by a bigger margin.

New Zealand were continually showing the indiscipline which has been the worst feature of their tour.

In the second-half England went off at a cracking pace when, from a rolling maul, Youngs broke to the open and slipped to Winterbottom, who came within a whisker of scoring. Then a magnificent plunge by Simpson saw England raking the ball back to produce the first serious three-quarter movement of the game, which put Slemen away for the corner. But he was caught two feet out by full-back Deans.

Another lunge by Winterbottom had the All Blacks defence at full stretch and Youngs got the ball away for Woodward to kick for the diagonal. England rolled from the line-out and Colclough powered his way over for a try which Hare converted to give England a two-score lead.

RUGBY FOOTBALL UNION

ENGLAND
v
NEW ZEALAND

TWICKENHAM
SATURDAY 19th NOVEMBER
1983

Official Programme
Fifty Pence

Secretary R.F.U.

Oti relishes trying times

The Sunday Times

Sunday, 20th March, 1988

By Norman Harris

It was probably the most extraordinary match that any of us at Twickenham had ever seen. Currents of tragedy and joy gave it a powerful sense of theatre, rousing emotions that were as remarkable in themselves as the stunning fact that in the second-half, England scored six tries to gain their biggest win over Ireland.

Three of those tries formed a hat-trick for Chris Oti who, certainly, will never forget the occasion. The reception he got after his third try was unprecedented, and an hour after the game two policemen had to escort him through the crowd that had filled the concourse under the main stand to pay him honour.

England were 3-0 down after a half which was almost as grey as the Twickenham skies. They had established no real control or rhythm, and had been embarrassed by losing the ball at the back of their scrum for Kiernan to exploit with a comfortable drop goal.

When the curtain went up on the second-half, England soon demonstrated to themselves – and perhaps to their sceptical coaches – just how easy it is to create the sort of space from which tries can be scored. Underwood was tackled just short of the line, his momentum nearly carried him over, but the forwards completed it anyway. Mr Norling indicated that it was Rees who had scored England's first try of the Championship.

Oti's advance to centre stage came after the forwards tried to smash their way over the Irish line. Harding had the intelligence to pass, as quickly and as far as possible, to the short side. Halliday passed just as quickly to Oti and the winger got home in the corner.

Twice more with the ball in hand, Oti was to humiliate the Irish defence, escaping on the inside as easily as on the outside. After his third try, he was given an ovation by spectators all around the ground as they stood clapping, hands high above their heads and then started singing – an event rare at Twickenham – 'Swing Low, Sweet Chariot'.

At the end, Underwood showed just what a dangerous player he is as he twisted the knife into a demoralised Irish defence by scoring England's fifth and sixth tries. It was an extremely novel way to avoid the wooden spoon.

RUGBY FOOTBALL UNION

ENGLAND
v
IRELAND

THE SAVE & PROSPER INTERNATIONAL

THE 100th MATCH

TWICKENHAM
SATURDAY 19th MARCH 1988

OFFICIAL PROGRAMME
£1·00
(Including 20p contribution to Charitable Trust)

SAVE & PROSPER
■ THE INVESTMENT HOUSE ■

Secretary R.F.U.

THE SAVE & PROSPER INTERNATIONAL

THE CHANGING
STADIUM

NORTH POINTS THE WAY

WHEN WILLIAM CAIL ENVISAGED A NEW, permanent home for English rugby, we can only imagine how he might have pictured the grand project in his mind before it became a reality. Whether the long-standing RFU Honorary Treasurer could ever have foreseen Twickenham as it stands today, a magnificent 82,000-capacity testament to his forward thinking, must remain a matter of conjecture.

The years that spanned the beginning of work on the ground back in 1907, as the original orchard and market garden in TW1 were unceremoniously cleared away, and the unveiling of the old 'new South Stand' in 1981 certainly saw sweeping changes to the famous stadium.

The dramatic transformation, however, was far from finished and if the 74 years between the first chapter in Twickenham's famous history and the opening of the 1981 South Stand saw a period of gradual evolution, the quarter-of-a-century that followed was an era of relative revolution.

The modern Twickenham began to take shape in the late 1980s as the RFU surveyed the stadium's ageing East, West and North Stands. The gleaming new stand at the south end of the ground merely highlighted their long years of loyal service and in June 1988 a firm of architects was appointed to design a new three-tier North Stand.

The original plans were for a 20,000-capacity structure with both seating and standing areas but the tragic loss of 96 lives at Hillsborough in April 1989 changed all that. Although the resulting Taylor Report that followed the disaster recommending all-seater stadia would not be published until the following year, the RFU could sense the wind of change and the design was changed to include 15,000 new seats and no terracing.

Demolition began in May 1989 and so down came Archibald Leitch's famous corrugated iron stand. At the same time, the old groundsman's cottage was flattened and with it the last physical remnant of the original 1909 ground was lost. Twickenham had truly entered into a new era.

Work on the new lower stand was completed in time for the Barbarians clash with New Zealand in late November 1989 and by 1990 the full North Stand was finished, boasting the longest cantilever roof in Britain. It also featured corporate boxes, reflecting the RFU's growing commercial awareness.

Above: An architectural drawing of the proposed new North stand

Bottom left: Princess Anne formally opens the new stand in 1991

Bottom right: Side view of the finished stand

Far right: Twickenham Stadium, pictured during the 1991 World Cup

RISING IN THE EAST

The foundations are laid for the new East Stand...

... and the new structure quickly emerges from the rubble

To create a somewhat lopsided Twickenham... albeit temporarily

WITH A NEW CAPACITY OF 75,000, in 1991 Twickenham welcomed the Rugby World Cup to London for the first time and although England narrowly lost in the final to Australia, the ever-changing stadium had made its bow on a truly global stage.

One lasting legacy of the 1991 tournament is the gleaming gold lion statue that adorns the Rowland Hill Memorial Gate. The lion had been in position for some 19 years before the World Cup came to Twickenham but in celebration of the landmark occasion it was given a very smart, pre-tournament coat of gold leaf at a cost of £6,000.

It was now time to address the issue of the existing East and West Stands. Although they both still had a life expectancy of a further 15 years, their new neighbours at the north and south ends of the ground made it obvious they would have to be rebuilt and as the World Cup was fading into memory, plans were drawn up for a new, £27million East Stand. It was to be followed by a £32million redevelopment on the opposite side of the pitch.

The first phase of the East Stand was completed by November 1992 with 10,500 seats installed in the lower tier and 12 months later it was completed as 68,000 supporters poured through the gates to watch England pull off a famous 15-9 victory over the All Blacks.

Attention now turned to erecting the new West Stand. Planning permission was successfully submitted in March 1994 and just days after that year's Middlesex Sevens final, the bulldozers once again rolled in to remove an edifice of Twickenham's past and pave the way for its future.

Right: The old West Stand is demolished in the summer of 1994

GO WEST

Bottom left: Phase two of the West Stand construction, well underway in 1995

Bottom right: Three-quarters of the way there!

Far right: England and South Africa run out for what would become the first ever floodlit match at Twickenham in 1995

THE SUMMER OF 1994 was a period of hectic building activity but by November 10,000 seats were available in the brand new West Stand (the new Royal Box was also ready) and they were christened by England fans as their side demolished Romania.

The second phase of the work was completed in the autumn of 1995 and as well as the full quota of seats, the West Stand now featured a state-of-the-art medical facility, fitness centre and the 'Spirit of Rugby' restaurant. Twickenham's 'concrete horseshoe', encompassing the new East, North and West Stands, was now proudly in place.

Another aspect of this flurry of building work saw floodlights installed at the stadium at a cost of £1million. Rugby in TW1 had been strictly limited to the daylight hours in the previous 86 years of the ground's history but the RFU could now illuminate proceedings and on 18th November England and recently-anointed world champions South Africa played on the famous turf in the full glare of the stadium's latest addition as the afternoon light faded. Unfortunately it was the Springboks and not England who found the new illumination more to their liking and the World Cup holders emerged 24-14 victors.

The following month the World Rugby Museum (then known as the Museum of Rugby) was opened, featuring the famed 'The Harry Langton Collection' of rugby memorabilia which charted the game's rich history and which the RFU had purchased specifically to fill its new attraction.

Three-quarters of Twickenham was now a thoroughly modern stadium but the aloof, detached South Stand suddenly looked incongruous next to its interlocking neighbours and although it was a mere 20-years-old, the RFU began to consider the possibility of consigning it to the dustbin of history and building a replacement that would complete the ground's iconic wraparound design.

LAST PIECE OF THE JIGSAW

BY SEPTEMBER 2002 THE AMBITIOUS PLANS had been finalised and the RFU announced its intention to erect a new South Stand that would bring the stadium's capacity to 82,000, a world record for a purpose-built rugby ground. The project was costed at £80million, complete with an integral hotel, and at the beginning of 2003 the proposals were submitted for planning permission.

It had taken six years in total to build the new North, East and West Stands but few at the RFU could have suspected that it would take a further six for the South Stand project to be completed.

The RFU had to work hard to allay the concerns of local residents and Richmond Council, as this was actually the first planning application to propose increasing the capacity of the stadium.

Another contentious elements of the plan was the necessity to demolish 22 Victorian and Edwardian villas – methodically purchased over the years by the RFU – to create enough space for the final project.

The RFU argued that the latest development would provide an annual £40 million boost to the local economy and the London of Chamber of Commerce were publicly enthusiastic but progress was slow and the 2003 World Cup in Australia came and went and with it the intended window of opportunity for the building work to begin.

In December 2003, after a lengthy consultation process with local residents, planning permission was granted. However, the RFU decided to review the plans to make sure it fitted in with their financial model, and early in 2004 they were resubmitted. The new plans featured a reduction in the height of the stand, 44 fewer hotel rooms and a reduction in the total floorspace of 16 per cent. The underground car park was also dropped but a £400,000 performing arts centre was retained.

The modifications were finally approved and, in early December 2004,

Below: Just 24 years old, the first new South Stand is reduced to rubble at the flick of a swich

Richmond Council's planning department finally gave the project the green light.

The next phase was demolition but the 5,000 tonnes of the South Stand's relatively young concrete and steel represented a formidable challenge to the contractors. It was eventually decided that explosives were needed in order to get the job done as quickly as possible and minimise the disruption to the surrounding area that would have resulted from the stand being torn down by mechanical methods.

The big day came on 10th July 2005 and after a brief eulogy from RFU President Elect LeRoy Angel and a minute's silence in memory of those who had lost their lives in the London bombings three days earlier, the switch was flicked and the South Stand came crashing down in a billowing cloud of dust.

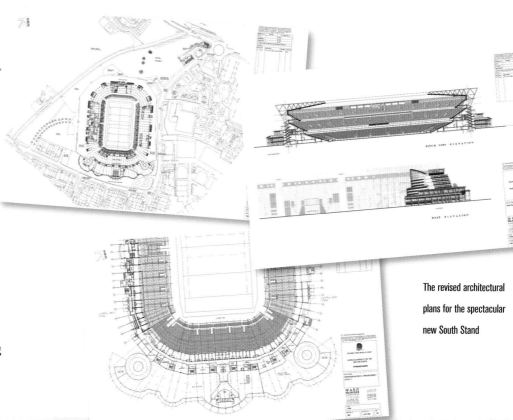

The revised architectural plans for the spectacular new South Stand

THE WORLD'S FINEST RUGBY STADIUM

AFTER ALMOST THREE YEARS OF DELAYS and frustration, the building work could now begin in earnest and, just 15 months after the demolition of the old structure, the new South Stand was finished and Twickenham was ready for the 82,000 supporters it could now accommodate. The stadium's flawless, wraparound design was in place.

It was fitting that the first country to face England in their new surroundings were the All Blacks, the touring team that had first convinced Cail that the RFU needed its own home more than a century ago, and although the men in white were unable to mark the occasion

with a victory, the majesty of the revamped ground struck all those who witnessed New Zealand's 40-21 triumph.

The stadium however was not yet quite complete. In November 2008 the new South Stand Rugby Store opened for business, in March the 2009 the London Marriott Hotel welcomed its first guests and in 2009 the treadmills began to roll in the impressive Virgin Active Classic gym.

The Home of England Rugby was now well and truly finished and Billy Williams' old 'Cabbage Patch' had been transformed into a 21st century cathedral of rugby.

The modern stadium - the largest purpose-built rugby stadium in the world - in all its glory as England take on Ireland in the Six Nations

Views of the impressive
new South Stand structure

The famous Hermes weather vane, first installed in place of the clock on the South Terrace in 1950, which now adorns the North Stand

The Rowland Hill Memorial Gate, also now known as Lion Gate for obvious reasons

The gold lion statue and one of the four rugby statues which welcome visitors to Twickenham

THE BEST LAID PLANS

TERRY WARD – PARTNER AT WARD McHUGH ASSOCIATES AND ARCHITECT WHO HAS BEEN INVOLVED IN THE DESIGN OF THE NEW NORTH, EAST, WEST AND SOUTH STANDS

"I WAS WORKING FOR A COMPANY called Husband & Co, based in Sheffield, when we won the contract to design the new North Stand in 1988. The RFU had a vision to create one of the finest sports stadiums in the world and they made it clear they wanted a design for the North Stand that could be replicated and rolled out to complete the ground's wraparound look that you see today.

"The RFU had considered selling up and rebuilding outside the M25 but in the end the Twickenham brand name was too valuable and they decided to redevelop and stay in London.

"I didn't have any particular design concept in mind at the outset but I did visit the Parc des Princes in Paris for some inspiration, which was a ground that really made the hairs stand up on the back of your neck on match days.

"The North Stand was the first full three-tier stand in the country. The lower tier was originally going to be terracing but that was shelved in the wake of the Hillsborough tragedy. If the terracing had been retained and incorporated in the other stands, the total capacity of Twickenham today would be 125,000.

"It was finished in time for the 1990/91 season and the World Cup. The highest seats were 100 feet above ground level, so we incorporated escalators and double spiral staircases, which were both fairly radical innovations for a sports stadium in those days.

"It was such a success that the RFU commissioned the East Stand after the World Cup finished and because the plan was always to complete the bowl, the West and finally the South Stands followed. It all had to be designed and built in phases because all the money came from the RFU's own coffers and there was no lottery money or government grant available to pay for everything to be done in one fell swoop.

"I think the end result is quite remarkable. Twickenham is the largest purpose-built rugby stadium in the world and compares to any other sporting venue. I don't think there's anywhere quite like it.

"My favourite part of the ground is the West Stand. The North and East were built as shells but the West was fitted out with dressing rooms, a medical suite, a gymnasium, the Spirit of Rugby restaurant, the Members' Bar, the President's Room, VIP suites and the England Rugby Internationals Club. It is also home to one of the ground's hidden gems – the Twickenham Cellar. The original idea came from Dudley Wood, the former RFU Secretary, who had a vision that, playing against the greatest wine-producing nations, he wanted a cellar in which he could store the world's best wines. So we incorporated a cellar deep into the stand. Tony Hallett, the ex-RFU Secretary, suggested we made it into a venue for entertaining and Twickenham now has a cellar and dining room that looks like something right out of *The Three Musketeers* (See *Behind the Scenes,* page 84).

"The ground also has some beautiful sculptures that people might miss on matchday, which I was keen to see being included in the redevelopment. The Rowland Hill Memorial Gate has four statues depicting players by sculptor Gerald Laing but probably less well-known is the modern, abstract piece called 'Union' by the singer Tommy Steele, which is located on one of the lift shafts on the East Stand. Steele is a keen rugby supporter and asked the RFU if he could produce something for the ground."

Epitomising the spirit of rugby come rain or shine

Vibrant display lifts England for title tilt

The Times

Monday, 7th November 1988

By David Hands

I must give up being a neutral observer if rugby matches keep turning out as this one at Twickenham on Saturday did. It is too uncomfortable squirming on a seat wondering until the closing seconds upon which of two horses to put one's money on.

Only when Halliday scored in the first minute of injury-time could England truly feel that this marvellous encounter was theirs, by three goals, a try and two penalty goals to two goals, a try and a penalty. It was a vibrant, sporting contest, well refereed, played in ideal conditions before as supportive a crowd as Twickenham has seen for many a day, not one of whom would have left early as Australia rallied at the last to try and snatch the brand from the fire.

They have, never, in 16 games, scored as many points against Australia and their doing so in such positive fashion prompted

Farr-Jones, the touring captain, to suggest England will contest with France the Five Nations in the New Year.

It was also a triumph of character, for twice in the game England fell behind because of self-inflicted wounds. The second was from Webb's pass that Campese, intercepting, galloped 60 metres to score at the beginning of the second-half. Television did not show the whole England team grouped round their young captain, Carling, under the posts as he steadied his troops and Lynagh prepared the conversion.

England rallied in the shape of Underwood, whose two tries in the same corner in which Oti scored his three against Ireland last season must make watchers in the north-west hospitality boxes feel coming to Twickenham is like Christmas. But if Underwood was the executioner-in-chief, the team build-up to both tries was immense.

It was fitting that Carling provided the final thrust. Probyn robbed Miller at a ruck and the centre made a decisive break, feeding Halliday before the collision with Leeds which removed him from the field. Halliday, in a clear field, cantered to the posts for his first try for the national side. November 5? Who needs fireworks?

Baa-Baas try as good as 1973 classic

Daily Express

Monday, 1st October 1990

By Tony Bodley

Neil Back, a husky 21-year-old Coventry insurance official, has become an overnight star in a film epic that will run and run. Blond-haired flanker Back featured twice in a stunning Barbarians try the 50,000 at Twickenham will never forget.

It ranks alongside Gareth Edwards' seven-man gem against New Zealand in Cardiff in 1973. That has been shown hundreds of times and now it has a worthy successor. It has already had more than 20 showings with newscasts and yesterday's *Rugby Special*.

The 66th minute touchdown lacked the three breathtaking side-steps by Phil Bennett to start the move, but it had pace, running and magical handling.

Australian scrum-half Nick Farr-Jones took a tap penalty. New Zealand prop Richard Loe drove on and the uncapped Auckland flanker Eric Rush found room with his phenomenal speed. Back took the ball in support and handed on to All Black powerhouse Joe Stanley who straightened the line.

David Campese, the world record Test try-scorer, almost ran out of space on the wing but threw the ball over his head inside to Back. He transferred the ball to Farr-Jones and Phil Davies thundered in to take the final pass and roar over after a move covering 90 yards.

The shaft of brilliance brought a standing ovation

and cut England's lead to six points. Back, who moved from Nottingham to Leicester in the summer, substituted for French flanker Karl Janik after 46 minutes. From the moment he announced his arrival with a crunching tackle on England skipper Will Carling, his perpetual motion kept him close to the ball.

Back has the most impressive fitness records of all of England's various squads. If Peter Winterbottom's rib injury is serious, team manager Geoff Cooke might gamble on him against Argentina in five weeks time.

The super try proved the Baa-Baas' last throw with their forwards mostly on their knees. But England, after shattered visions of glory in the last two seasons, should have wiped out the opposition instead of a dodgy 18-16 victory.

Carling, a forlorn figure after the Grand Slam failure against Scotland and almost lost for words after losing the Second Test in Argentina, must be haunted by fears of another year of unfulfilled potential.

Neither Underwood brother got on the score-sheet but Rory made a monkey out of Campese setting up Simon Hodgkinson's try.

TWICKENHAM
TREASURES

THE WORLD RUGBY MUSEUM

AS WELL AS BEING THE WORLD'S FOREMOST RUGBY stadium, Twickenham also houses the finest collection of rugby memorabilia on the planet.

From the first ever laws of the game, handwritten in 1871, to the ball used in the 2003 World Cup final, the World Rugby Museum – opened in 1996 in the brand new East Stand – is crammed with rugby history.

Much more than that, the museum is an inspirational interactive journey through the history of the ultimate team game. Having entered through the original Twickenham turnstiles, the innovative exhibits bring some of the game's great moments to life with the help of sights, sounds and even smells from the very earliest days of rugby right up to the modern era.

Some of the 'treasures' from the World Rugby Museum are on display over the next few pages, but nothing beats a visit in person. On non-matchdays, entry to the museum is included in the museum's high quality Stadium Tours, on matchdays it is open from 11am to all match ticket holders.

For further information or to book a tour visit www.rfu.com/museum or telephone 0208 892 8877.

TWICKENHAM
WORLD RUGBY MUSEUM

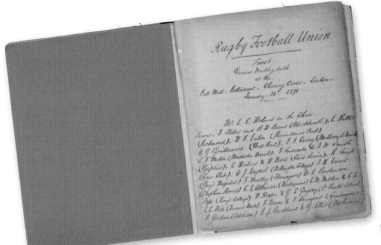

The original minutes from the meeting in 1871 at the Pall Mall Restaurant, London, that led to the formation of the Rugby Football Union

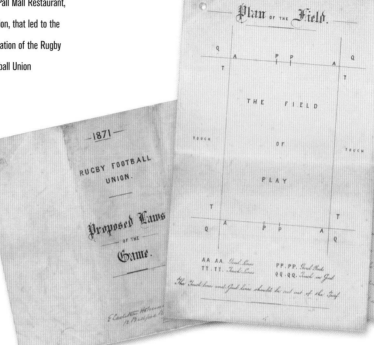

Hand-written draft of the first ever 'Laws' of rugby, again from 1871 ➤

A silver medal from the 1908 Olympic Games in London when Great Britain, represented by Cornwall, were beaten by Australia

A cap and shirt from England's first ever international match – indeed the first ever rugby international – against Scotland at Raeburn Place in Edinburgh in 1871

◄ The stunning Calcutta Cup, in residence at Twickenham only when England are victorious over Scotland in the Championship

Poster advertising Middlesex's midweek clash with the All Blacks at Stamford Bridge, home of Chelsea Football Club, during their famous 1905 tour ➤

The hand-embroidered touch judge's flag from England's drawn match with South Africa at Crystal Palace in 1906 ⩔

◄ New Zealand shirt worn on their 1905 'Originals' tour of Britain

◄ France shirt, circa 1912

England Schoolboys' shirt worn in the first international fixture against their Wales counterparts in 1905 ➤

Wales shirt from 1912 season ➤

↗ A pre-1871 'football' from the days

before the laws of 'rugby' were formalised

↗ A rugby ball dating from the mid 20th century

↗ A ball from England's 1957 Grand Slam

season, presented to captain Eric Evans

↗ A ball used on Australia's Grand Slam tour of Britain

and Ireland in 1984, signed by the entire Australian squad

One of several balls used during the 2003 World Cup final in Sydney, signed by match referee Andre Watson ➤

The International Rugby Football Board

The Webb Ellis Cup

◄ The three-quarter size replica of the Webb Ellis Cup, presented to England after their victory over Australia in the World Cup final in 2003

GILBERT
XACT SIZE : 5
RUGBY WORLD CUP FINAL
22ND NOVEMBER 2003
SYDNEY

1987 NEW ZEALAND
1991 AUSTRALIA
1995 SOUTH AFRICA
1999 AUSTRALIA
2003 ENGLAND

An original oil painting of Kathleen Trick, the daughter of a London Welsh committee member, wearing kit gifted to her by the 1906 touring Springboks

The official New Zealand mascot of the 1970s ➢

⋏ The original tactics board used on the British & Irish Lions tour of Australia and New Zealand in 1950

The personal mascot of Newport forward Robert Dibble from the unofficial Anglo-Welsh Lions tour of Australia and New Zealand in 1908 ➢

◄ A distinctive South Africa blazer
from the 1906 tour of Britain

◄ An official 'RFU' England blazer

An All Blacks blazer from the 1970s ➤

◄ A British & Irish Lions blazer from the
1966 tour of Australia & New Zealand

ENGLAND 21
FRANCE 19

Saturday, 16th March 1991

LAND OF HOPE AND GLORY!

The Times

Monday, 18th March 1991

By Colin Price

As England fans partied through the weekend to celebrate a first Grand Slam for 11 years, the players' minds raced ahead to the World Cup in October. The inquest into a sensational showdown, however, between two unbeaten sides of contrasting styles will reveal one stark fact. England, whatever control is achieved through their mighty pack, can kiss the World Cup goodbye

if they continue to be as vulnerable to sides that counter-attack as brilliantly as the French.

Serge Blanco, in his championship farewell, should have set the alarm bells ringing by sparking the greatest try of all time when he caught England napping by running from behind his own try-line.

And Will Carling's men were left hopelessly exposed again two minutes from time when Philippe Sella and Blanco brilliantly fashioned a try by Franck Mesnel which silenced the deafening strains of 'Sweet Chariot'.

In between, Carling and Dean Richards got into a tangle trying to field an up and under from Didier Camberabero to give the fly-half a gift follow-up try.

That added up to three tries to one for the French and once again the difference was Simon Hodgkinson's boot which survived an attack of nerves to land 14 points for a new championship record of 60 points.

When England shrugged off that brilliant 12th minute Philippe Saint-Andre try to lead 18-9 at half-time the drenched crowd sat back waiting for a feast.

Instead, the French still found the kind of opportunity Carling had sought to eliminate by screwing the lid down so firmly.

Camberabero, whose magic helped Blanco fashion the first score, kicked high to the right of the England posts. Carling appeared to have it covered until Richards came thundering in, the ball fell loose and Camberabero gleefully picked up for one of the easiest tries of his career.

But England just kept their nerve and clung on to wipe out the ghosts of two years of heartbreak and failure.

France, however, returned home with the memory of scoring a better try even than Gareth Edwards' famous effort for the Barbarians against New Zealand.

Blanco began it by running a missed Hodgkinson penalty from behind his own line. In a blur of speed, Sella took it on down the touchline. Camberabero raced through, chipped over Underwood and gathered in one stride then cross-kicked perfectly for Saint-Andre to complete the move.

Dallaglio leads his England heroes into rugby's fast lane

The Independent

Monday, 8th December 1997

By Chris Hewett

Thirty-six hours on in the bleak light of the Monday morning after the Saturday afternoon before, it is still tempting to wallow in the euphoria of it all. Confronted by the sporting equivalent of the Black Death, the red rose army not only survived, but flourished. They were a revelation: passionate, fierce, vital, dynamic, vivacious. And that was only the crowd. The players were better than that. Far, far better.

Yes, the new emotionalists of Twickenham saw England take a moon-step along the road to possible World Cup glory at the weekend; yes, Clive Woodward can now proceed in the knowledge that his visions and theories are the stuff of hard reality rather than science fiction. But when all is said and done, England drew a match they should have won against a side not so much on its knees after ten months of relentless activity, but flat on its back.

When Woodward views the video of this momentous Twickenham occasion – and he will be quite justified in watching it ad nauseam – he will take enormous encouragement from three particular aspects. The first and most tangible of them was England's second try, scored after nine minutes by the outstanding Richard Hill, but created, quite beautifully, by Paul Grayson, Austin Healey and Will Greenwood.

Secondly, England now know they possess a footballing back row of undisputed world class. If Hill was sensational on Saturday – good enough to produce a try-saving tackle on Norm Hewitt at one end before giving the fast-retreating Jeff Wilson a serious dose of the heebie-jeebies at the other – Lawrence Dallaglio and Neil Back were scarcely less effective. Their collective expertise meant that Taine Randell had to perform a whole range of heroics to keep the tourists at the races early on, while Josh Kronfeld was press-ganged into one of the most accomplished 40 minutes of his career after the interval.

And the third bonus? The raw spirit that allowed England to spend 30 second-half minutes on the ropes, dust themselves down and tear into the last ten with a ferocity so conspicuous by its absence against the Springboks seven days previously. Roger Uttley, the manager, was right when he compared an epic finale to the conclusion of perfectly matched prize fight.

FIELD OF DREAMS

THE HALLOWED TURF

IF YOU THINK OF TWICKENHAM'S ELEGANT, imposing stands as the frame, the verdant grass they surround is undoubtedly the masterpiece at the heart of HQ. The stadium may have undergone many dramatic changes in its century of staging top-class rugby but the pitch has remained the ground's crowning glory, making a mockery of the sceptics who argued Billy Williams's patch of land would never be fit for purpose.

Even the completion of the ground's eye-catching but potentially cloying wraparound design in 2006 has failed to dull the famed turf and while a litany of other modern sporting stadia have experienced teething problems with their own green stuff, the Twickenham pitch today has never looked better.

The process of creating a world-class playing surface began even before the old East and West Stands were built and owed much to the foresight of Charles Arnold Crane, President of the RFU between 1907 and 1909. Fears about flooding from the nearby River Crane had lingered since the RFU first purchased the site but Crane took the decision to allow the contractors building the Metropolitan Underground line to dump their spoil at the ground and so raise the pitch level a full two feet.

A herringbone drainage system – named after its angular resemblance to a fish skeleton – was also installed and Twickenham was almost ready for its inaugural match. All that was required was someone to mark out the pitch.

The history books name Charlie Hale as HQ's first groundsman but the Twickenham annals also reveal that the RFU sought outside help in 1909 before the stadium hosted Harlequins against Richmond in October.

"Mr George Street," read the telegram sent to the then Blackheath groundsman from the RFU Secretary. "Could you or your son come over on Tuesday with measuring lines and give my man a hand in marking out the Ground? Yours sincerely, Charles Marriott."

There is no further mention of George Street in the RFU minutes but with the whitewash duly applied, the ground was ready for the Quins match and a new era for English rugby.

The playing surface, however, received a mixed reception from the media. "The turf is excellent," enthused H. Vincent Jones in *The Observer* while, in contrast, *The Thames Valley Times* reported, "the grass was a little long for fast football, but surely Mr Marriott, the conscientious secretary and manager of the ground, will put this right by next Saturday."

Although the Duke of Northumberland's river did break its banks in 1927 and flooded the West Car Park, the pitch itself was spared a watery fate and for the next 20 years the ground enjoyed a reputation as one of the finest fields in the game.

Far right: Rugby's most famous turf in fine fettle prior to the commencement of hostilities

Right: George Street and the note summoning him to mark out the lines for Twickenham's first match

Rugby Football Union.

TELEGRAPHIC ADDRESS: "Scrummage, Twickenham."

TWICKENHAM.

7 - 9 - 09

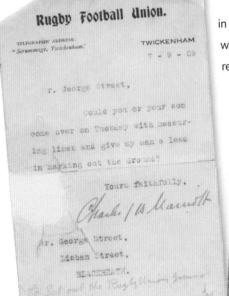

By 1958, when England played Ireland, the state of the pitch was a cause of considerable concern

NOT SO GLORIOUS MUD

THERE WERE, HOWEVER, PROBLEMS on the horizon in the post-Second World War years as Twickenham became a victim of its own success. More and more matches – not least an average of 18 Harlequins fixtures – were being held at the ground each season and as a result the pitch began to show increasing signs of wear and tear. The deteriorating state of the original drainage system merely exacerbated the situation and HQ began to acquire an unwanted reputation for muddy conditions.

In 1953 the RFU called in W H Bowles, the Chairman of the National Association of Groundsmen, to assess the problems but it was not until 1964 and the appointment of Harold Clark as Twickenham's Clerk of Works and Ground Superintendent that the situation was decisively addressed.

A typically no-nonsense Yorkshireman, Clark had previously worked for British Rail in Leeds and was singularly unimpressed on his first visit to HQ as he assessed the scale of the challenge ahead of him.

"On arrival at Twickenham, I had my first view of what was known in the north as the notorious 'Twickenham Bog'," Clark wrote. "At the east and west scrummaging areas in rainy periods, there was standing water in the turf which during matches turned into a sea of mud to ankle depth.

"We eventually came under the South Terrace and into the ground staff mess that turned out to be an old urinal. On the floor, there were several men, laid with coats over them asleep. I realised they were drunk. I asked who they were and they told me they were part of my staff and it was usual to steal beer before any match when it was on the premises."

Clark may have been tempted to turn to the bottle himself but instead decided to dig up the entire pitch and install a revolutionary new drainage system. His chief innovation as the work began was to create slits filled with sand just beneath the playing surface to allow surface water to drain away as quick as possible which, coupled with his reluctance to compact the soil with heavy rollers, ensured Twickenham became dry once again.

Water of course was not the only danger to play. Frost and snow constantly threatened to disrupt the fixture list in the winter months and whenever the forecast suggested an untimely cold snap, Twickenham was immediately bedecked with a blanket of straw to insulate the grass.

The winter of 1952 was particularly inclement and some 20 tonnes of straw were strewn across the HQ turf to ensure England's game with South Africa could go ahead. It took three hours on the morning of the game to remove the temporary covering and any unsuspecting supporter who arrived at the ground too early was unceremoniously press-ganged into helping with the removal effort.

Later in the decade, Twickenham started using a contraption called the 'Jetaire Space Heater', essentially an oversized hair dryer, to blow hot air under tarpaulins placed on top of the grass to combat the threat of frost. Whilst this more often than not had the desired effect, by the time the coverings and straw had been removed the playing surface underneath was often not much more than a treacly mess.

Nevertheless, in a century of rugby at HQ, only two Tests – against France in 1947 and Scotland 40 years later – have had to be postponed due to the worst excesses of the British weather.

Above top: Straw was often used to combat frost

Above: By the late fifties groundstaff employed heaters to stop the pitch from freezing

KENT, THE GARDENER OF ENGLAND

KEITH KENT –
HEAD GROUNDSMAN

Above: Keith Kent and his team, Ian Ayling and Andy Muir

Below: Every year the pitch is re-seeded

"**I**'VE BEEN THE HEAD GROUNDSMAN at Twickenham since September 2002. I worked for Manchester United at Old Trafford for 15 years before I took the job here, so I suppose you could say I'm familiar with the challenge of looking after pitches surrounded by big, modern stadia.

"The biggest challenge I've faced here came with the completion of the South Stand in 2006 because that completely enclosed the ground and we had to deal with the problems of a lack of natural light and wind. The stands are so high that much of the west side of the pitch is in shade from midday through the winter months.

"We solved that problem in 2005 with a portable lighting system developed by a Dutch company called Stadium Grow Lighting. A guy from Rotterdam came up with the technology for growing roses in greenhouses. It was so successful he was apparently producing 40,000 roses for sale every day, 365 days a year and it has worked wonders here.

"The system is a series of artificial growing lamps on long metal arms, which are mounted on wheel bases so we can move them around the pitch, depending on which areas need light.

"We always knew a lack of wind would also be an issue and when the South Stand was being designed, I spoke at length with RFU about how we could alleviate the problem. We came up with a series of louvres (or slats) in the south-east and south-west corners of the ground, which we can open up to increase air flow.

"A lot of modern stadia import their turf on pallets but the fixture list at Twickenham means we can reseed every year in the summer, which is a

huge advantage. I always say that grass grown in Yorkshire and then suddenly laid in an alien environment is going to be in a state of shock.

"The grass here has deeper roots because it was actually grown here. It develops accustomed to the shade, to the overall conditions and it's stronger and more resilient as a result.

"There is no undersoil heating at Twickenham but, fingers crossed, we're confident we can handle anything the weather throws at us. We have a company on standby to supply covers and heaters for the autumn internationals and the Six Nations if there is a threat of snow or frost.

"We also have a direct line to the weatherman John Kettley. He's our little insurance policy and is always on hand to let us know if we need to get the covers on. The only situation that would cause us major problems would be a heavy snowfall on the morning of a match.

"The most hectic time I've experienced since I came to Twickenham was in August 2006 when we had the Middlesex Sevens, the Rolling Stones and the Rugby League Challenge Cup final on successive weekends.

"The Sevens finished on Saturday and that evening we had removed the turf at the end of south end of the pitch to make way for the aluminium flooring that was the base for the 450-tonne stage for the Stones concerts on the Sunday and Tuesday nights.

"The Stones played two nights, by eight o'clock on the Wednesday night we'd cleared the pitch and by end of play Thursday, we'd relaid the pitch for the Challenge Cup between St Helens and Huddersfield and everything was ready for a 2.30 kick-off on Saturday.

"It was a huge logistical challenge but we pulled it off."

Above: Artificial lighting keeps the grass growing even during the winter playing season

The Guardian

Monday, 1st November 1999

By Robert Kitson

The percussive sound of pompous theories being pricked accompanied France's team bus to Cardiff yesterday. All those pre-prepared essays on southern hemisphere invincibility, French disunity and worldwide unease about rugby's baffling law book lay scattered on the hard shoulder beside a New Zealand team still not quite sure what hit them. Back at Twickenham bits of Kiwi jawbone were still being picked off the floor.

For France's stunning win over the All Blacks was the sporting equivalent of the Titanic getting the better of the iceberg, the sledgehammer losing to the nut. For a World Cup in danger of toppling off its narrow ridge on the cliff-face of international affairs, it was almost too good to be true. When Bill McLaren describes Sunday's spectacular as the greatest game of rugby he has ever seen, there can be simply no doubting France's achievement.

The burning question since has been, 'How did they do that?' How did a side with

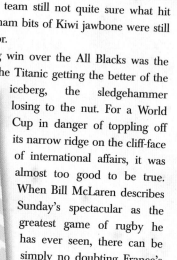

RUGBY WORLD CUP 1999 / RYGBI CWPAN Y BYD 1999

NEW ZEALAND v FRANCE

Semi-Final
Sunday 31st October 1999
Twickenham – Kick-off 3.00pm
Official Souvenir Programme £4.00

FFR

La Marseillaise rallies a nation

an awful recent track record, simmering internal discontent and, according to the distinguished former international Thierry Lacroix, no previous discernible gameplan, leave John Hart, the mouth from the south, clutching for words at the post-match press conference like a drowning man in a duckpond?

There was more to Sunday's result, though, than high notes and rousing calls to arms. The gung-ho French managed to achieve what England and Scotland have failed to do consistently, forcing the All Blacks to turn and tackle, isolating their back three and pressing the callow New Zealand pack on to the back foot.

The New Zealand coach may be backing the Wallabies in Saturday's final yet the Australians will already be re-examining the video with concern. Magne would have blasted holes in any side on the day but was that the same Fabien Galthie who used to look the most ponderous scrum-half in world rugby?

As for Christophe Dominici, the jinking sprinter from Stade Francais, can small really still be beautiful out wide where the big boys now roam? Those who insist the French cannot possibly reproduce their Twickenham masterpiece should also heed the words of their No8 Christophe Juillet. "If it's dry and sunny in Cardiff, nobody will stop us".

Valiant French subdued

The Sunday Telegraph
Sunday, 8th April 2001
By Paul Ackford

England march on. The final scoreline may have been horribly cruel to France but no-one can deny another quite outstanding performance from this England side. Six tries in all, five of them in a dazzling second-half onslaught. It took the breath away.

And again the records tumbled. This was England's highest score against France and Jonny Wilkinson confirmed, as we knew he would, his position as England's leading points scorer of all time, eclipsing his Newcastle mentor, Rob Andrew. Wilkinson fluffed his first chance to break the record but every other kick

went over and he has reached his milestone in 27 appearances for his country, whereas it took Andrew 71.

But England will draw even more satisfaction from the manner in which they eventually came good because this was a French side hugely motivated by the criticism they had received from their president, Bernard Lapasset, and it was a French side who, for 65 minutes at least, were true to their great traditions.

It was the fact that England were able to soak up France's excellence and rebut it so decisively at the end which was so impressive. In many ways, the game echoed the run-out against Italy earlier

in the Six Nations, when England struggled to contain a ferociously committed side but eventually came through strongly.

The man who eventually kick-started England was Richard Hill. The flanker has long been a mainstay of this England team. Understated and unexpressive, he rarely leaves a match without altering it significantly and yesterday was no exception. Hill opened England's second-half account when he charged to the line after Matt Dawson had taken a quick tap penalty. Hill has never been noted for his speed over the ground but he outpaced the French defence, finally dragging Jean-Luc Sadourny over the line. That score took England into a 18-16 lead and proved the launch pad for four further tries in a second period in which England scored a staggering 35 points and France managed only three.

There is little doubt now that this England side are the finest this country has produced and are on a par with some of the great British and Irish teams in history. A Grand Slam decider against Ireland in Dublin is next up.

TERRIFIC TRIES

PRINCE ALEXANDER OBOLENSKY

V NEW ZEALAND, 4TH JANUARY 1936

FEW PLAYERS ENJOY SUCH A REVERED PLACE in the folklore of the game than Alexander Obolensky, or 'Obo' as he was known by his team-mates, an exiled Russian prince who played just a handful of Test matches for his adopted homeland but whose place as an England legend was sealed by a moment of magic against the mighty New Zealand.

The huge Twickenham crowd rises to applaud Obolensky's moment of magic

Born in St Petersburg, the son of a serving Tsarist cavalry officer fled Russia to escape the Revolution of 1917 and settled in north London. By the age of 19 he was studying at Oxford when he was selected to make his debut for his adopted country against the touring All Blacks.

There had only been two previous Tests between the two countries.

New Zealand had won both but hopes were high ahead of kick-off at Twickenham that England could avoid a hat-trick of defeats.

Obolensky's impact on proceedings was nothing less than spectacular and if the crowd thought his first try of the match was a collector's item, they had seen nothing yet.

That first score saw the England right wing take Peter Cranmer's pass inside his own half and outpace the All Black defence but moments before the half-time whistle, Obolensky eclipsed his earlier score with a sublime effort that left the Kiwis trailing in his wake.

An initial break by Cranmer built up the momentum. Fly-half Peter Candler was in support to take an inside ball and he in turn passed to Obolensky, who was 30 metres from the line near the right touchline.

The wing momentarily paused to assess his options but rather than set off down the line as he had earlier, he cut back on the angle from right to left. The decision seemed to take New Zealand completely by surprise and Obolensky scythed through their lines and past a succession of Kiwis who were unable to pull him down.

The line was now at his mercy but All Black wing Neville Mitchell was racing valiantly across to cover. Obolensky accelerated and Mitchell dived but it was too late to stop him and the Twickenham faithful had witnessed a moment of true magic, not to mention an historic 13-0 English victory.

Tragically, Obolensky played just three more matches for England. He was killed in 1940 at the age of 24 when his Hurricane Hawker plane crashed during a training flight.

It was a premature end to an eventful life but the flying Russian had at least left an indelible mark on Twickenham with his stunning two-try salvo.

THE INSPIRATION FOR THE NAME of the eponymous character in Bernard Cornwell's famed Napoleonic Wars sagas, the rugby-playing Sharp is one of the elite band of captains to have led England to Championship glory. He achieved it in true storybook style too, scoring the decisive try at HQ to seal victory over Scotland and earn his place in the pantheon of the game's great leaders.

A game that was to become fondly known as 'Sharp's Match', the Calcutta Cup clash of 1963 was the final game of that season's Five Nations. England were defending a 12-year unbeaten record against their oldest rivals and although they could not claim the Grand Slam after a pointless draw with Ireland earlier in the

campaign, the traditional sense of anticipation as the two teams took to the field was undiminished.

Scotland scored first through burly flanker Ron Glasgow. England replied with a Nick Drake-Lee score but a conversion and a drop goal from Ken Scotland gave the visitors a slender advantage and the home side could sense the Championship trophy slipping through their fingers.

And so the skipper took matters into his own hands. England were awarded a scrum 40 metres from the Scottish line and possession was safely secured. The ball was shepherded back to scrum-half Simon Clarke who span it out in orthodox fashion to Sharp. But what followed was anything but orthodox.

England centre Mike Weston now came looming into view on a pre-arranged scissors move but he was merely a decoy runner and, just as the Scots realised they had been duped, Sharp set off.

Flanker Kenneth Ross was the first defender to be left trailing in the England captain's slipstream but his prospects of bursting through the obstacle that was the Scotland midfield partnership of David White and Brian Henderson looked remote until a sublime dummy and a timely burst of pace took him clear.

The Scottish full back Colin Blaikie was now all that stood between him and the line but it seemed certain Sharp would pass to England left wing Jim Roberts, who had appeared in support on his shoulder. Blaikie was faced with the dreaded two-on-one but Sharp sensed the full back was drifting wide to cover Roberts and opted for another perfectly-executed dummy. Scotland scrum half Stanley Coughtrie made one last despairing attempt to stop him but Sharp was over for a spectacular try that sealed a 10-8 triumph and his enduring place in the annals of HQ.

ANDY HANCOCK

V SCOTLAND, 20TH MARCH 1965

SOME GREAT TRIES ARE DESTINED to illuminate epic contests, providing the dramatic climax to a sumptuous feast of rugby. Others, however spectacular in their own right, prove to be rare gems in otherwise drab, tedious encounters.

Andy Hancock's wonderful try was witnessed by The Queen herself

Andy Hancock's score against the Scots falls firmly in the latter category. Not even the most myopic Calcutta Cup enthusiast would describe the 1965 clash between the old enemies as a classic but the 65,000 fans who did watch the largely turgid, mud-clad encounter at

Twickenham at least had the considerable consolation of witnessing one of the finest tries in the history of the famous old stadium.

Scotland had taken a 3-0 lead courtesy of a David Chisholm drop goal and after 79 minutes of play England had found no reply and were facing the real prospect of a first home defeat to the Scots in 27 years.

With the clock ticking, England seemed bereft of inspiration and invention but as Scotland pressed deep inside the 22, the ball squirted unexpectedly out of a maul. England fly half Mike Weston reacted quickest, seizing on the loose possession and feeding Hancock to his left, who had a mere 90 metres between him and the line.

He assessed his options and decided to go for broke. Scotland captain and full back Stewart Wilson and centre Iain Laughlan failed to get to him and Hancock was now in full flow as he accelerated ominously down the left touchline.

Scrum half Alexander Hastie came flying across but was beaten for pace but both Wilson and Laughlan were streaming back to cover with Hancock halfway there.

Wilson was the first to get back at the wing. England flanker Derek Rogers was valiantly trying to get up in support but Hancock beat Wilson single-handedly, turning the Scots' 15 inside out with a dazzling step and although Laughlan was breathing down his neck, he had just enough speed and, just as importantly, stamina to get over the line and level the scores at the death.

England missed the conversion that would have clinched victory and the match was drawn 3-3, but Hancock's spectacular solo effort ensured that the England faithful went home with smiles on their faces.

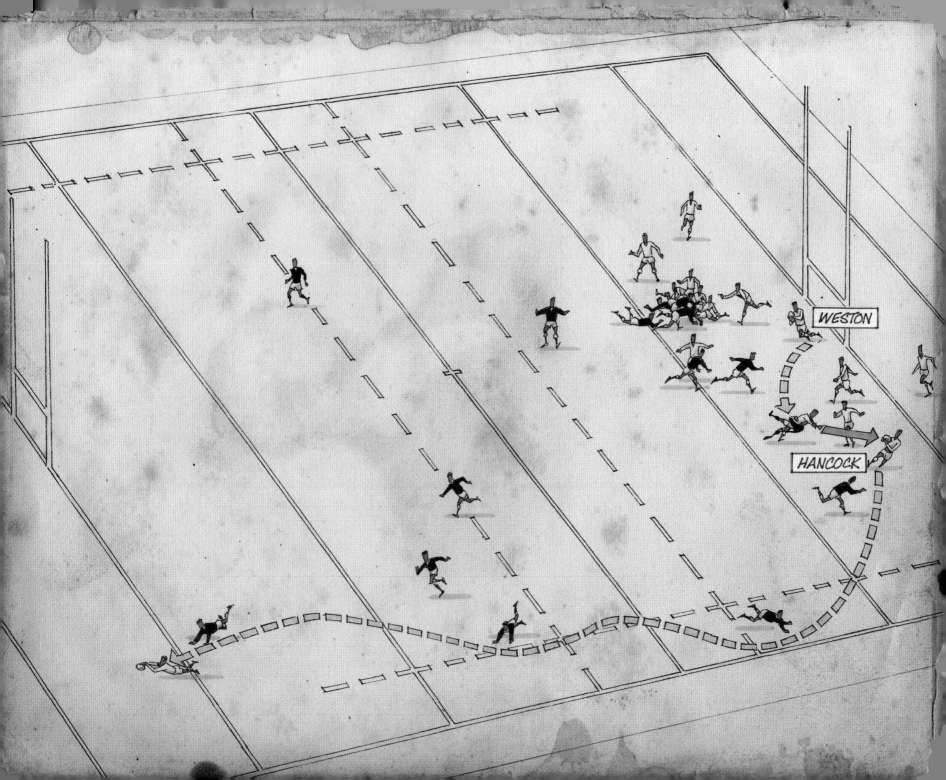

PETER DIXON

V SCOTLAND, 17TH MARCH 1973

WHEN ENGLAND TOOK TO THE FIELD against Scotland in March 1973, it can have been with no little trepidation or anxiety. The men in white had won just once in their previous eight outings at Twickenham and they had also failed to beat the Scots in any of their past four encounters.

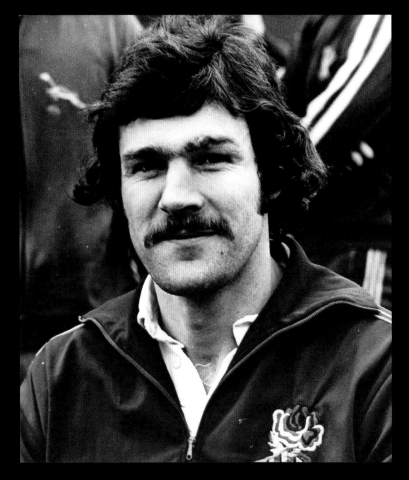

England's try-scoring hero Peter Dixon

In short, the omens were not good and the beleaguered home side were in dire need of inspiration, if not a victory. Mercifully, both were to arrive in the nick of time in the shape of Harlequins flanker Peter John Dixon.

The embryonic stages of the all-important try he was to eventually score – the spark for a morale-boosting 20-13 English victory – began on the halfway line and a Colin Telfer restart for the Scots.

His kick was gratefully gathered by the England second row Chris Ralston and before wayward Scottish hands could disrupt possession, he tossed the ball from above his head like a basketball player to his scrum-half Steve Smith. England were up and running.

Smith fed fly-half Martin Cooper who grubber kicked behind the onrushing Scotland midfield. A moment's hesitation allowed centre Geoff Evans to regain possession and, now deep in the opposition half, England could sense they had a real chance.

From Evans the ball went to David Duckham and the wing tore down the left-hand touchline to give the attack real momentum and menace. Scottish wings David Shedden and then William Steele managed to slow him down but before he was finally halted, he passed inside to Cooper, who in turn found Peter Preece.

The centre appeared to be covered but just as the move looked in danger of fizzling out as the Scottish defenders raced back into position, there was Dixon, charging up in support like any flanker worth his salt.

Forgoing any thoughts of subtlety, Dixon opted for the direct option, put his head down and attempted to drive the remaining three metres to the Scottish line. He might well have got their on his own but the rest of the England forwards were taking no chances and as they lent their collective weight to the maul, Dixon was propelled over for a famous score.

CLIVE WOODWARD

V SCOTLAND, 21ST FEBRUARY 1981

TO THE MORE YOUTHFUL GENERATIONS of English rugby supporters, Sir Clive Woodward is synonymous with that famous, unforgettable night in Sydney in 2003 when England finally broke the southern hemisphere stranglehold on the World Cup and triumphantly lifted the William Webb Ellis Trophy.

Perhaps better remembered as England coach, Sir Clive was also a fine player in his day

To the more gnarled followers of the fortunes of the men in white, plain old Clive as he was known in his playing days was a stylish centre for club (Leicester) and country, brimming with guile, pace and ambition.

A veteran of 21 Tests for England, Woodward's finest individual moment on the international stage came in 1981 against Scotland at Twickenham and his try in a 23-17 victory spoke volumes about the player's natural grace and poise.

The move that led to the score began with a routine, if hugely effective, England lineout. Hooker Peter Wheeler found skipper Bill Beaumont with a low, fast throw and the pack drove on to present Steve Smith with the kind of clean, crisp possession that scrum-halves dream of.

Smith's diving, bullet pass to the left to fly-half Huw Davies set the England backs in motion and Woodward, still some 35 metres out, came ghosting in from the left on the scissors. Davies found him with a neat reverse offload but two Scottish defenders stood guard, only to be left in his wake after a mesmerising step and swivel of the hips.

There was now space ahead of him and Woodward glided forward on a devastating angle from left to right to reach the Scottish 22. There was still work to do but the next hopeful tackler was taken out of the equation with a beautiful dummy and there were only two Scots remaining between him and the line.

Wing Bruce Hay had the pace to compete but Woodward beat him with a scintillating step inside off his right foot before jinking back out wide. Despite his valiant effort, flanker Jim Calder just didn't have the raw speed to deny the Englishman a dazzling solo try as he dived over in the corner.

WOODWARD

DAVIES

PHILIPPE SAINT-ANDRE (FRANCE)

V ENGLAND, 16TH MARCH 1991

ENGLAND'S FIVE NATIONS CLASH WITH FRANCE in 1991 was one of the greatest contests ever to have graced the stadium and although the record books will forever testify to a nail biting 21-19 victory for the men in white, the game's undisputed magic moment belonged to the French and, in particular, Philippe Saint-Andre.

Phillipe Saint-Andre gallops home to score Twickenham's greatest ever try... so far

Prosaic is not a word commonly, if ever, associated with Les Bleus and so it proved as they conjured up one of the most remarkable tries witnessed in TW1, galloping the entire length of the pitch and in the process leaving 15 bemused Englishmen chasing shadows.

It all began with the visitors on their own try line. The great Serge Blanco fielded Simon Hodgkinson's failed penalty attempt but it seemed madness to contemplate anything other than a pressure-relieving kick to touch. Blanco, of course, rarely did anything by the book and instead decided to pass to Jean-Baptiste Lafond, who also eschewed the safe option and moved the ball on to Philippe Sella.

To this point, it was all very eye-catching and cavalier but Sella was still deep in his own half, isolated towards the right touchline and, faced with hordes of English players ahead of him, seemingly going nowhere.

The French evidently saw things differently. Sella headed straight for prop Jeff Probyn, took the tackle and offloaded to fly half Didier Camberabero, who continued forward but perilously close to the touchline. England appeared to have him safely corralled but the French number ten was no easy catch and delicately chipped the ball over the onrushing Rory Underwood, collected it and looked up.

Flanker Laurent Cabannes was steaming up in support but Camberabero had another idea and launched what initially looked like an aimless, lateral kick into midfield. The sceptics cannot have seen Saint-Andre ghosting into the very same space and as he waited patiently for what he hoped would be a favourable bounce of the ball, the wing had the freedom of Twickenham.

A rugby ball can be a fickle mistress when it meets the turf but on this occasion fortune favoured the Frenchman and it bounced obediently into his hands, allowing him to set off on a 15-metre dash to crown a glorious French attack. Jeremy Guscott suddenly came into the picture and desperately tried to crash the party but Saint-Andre had too much of a headstart and he glided over underneath the posts.

Once again, the brilliant French had turned base metal into gold and conjured a try from nothing, and in 2009 this try was voted the greatest scored at HQ in Twickenham's first 100 years.

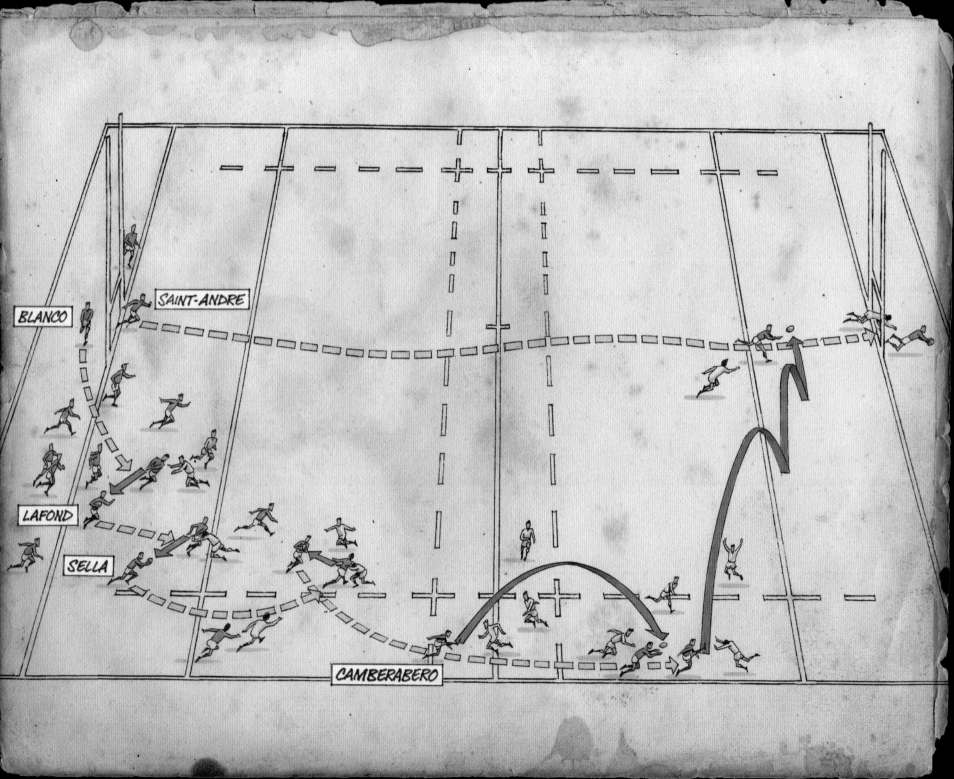

BLANCO

SAINT-ANDRE

LAFOND

SELLA

CAMBERABERO

RORY UNDERWOOD

THERE WERE FEW GREATER SIGHTS in the late 1980s and early 1990s than that of Rory Underwood scorching down the wing for England and many of his record-breaking 49 Test match tries were dazzling solo efforts that gloriously showcased his searing pace and unerring, predatory eye for the line.

Rory Underwood scored 49 Test match tries, including this beauty against Wales at Twickenham

Ironic then that his score against the Welsh in 1994 was a classic example of a 'team try' with Underwood supplying the turbo-charged coup de grace to a flowing English attack that ripped the Wales defence asunder and paved the way for a third successive victory at Twickenham over their Principality rivals.

The move began sedately just inside the England half. Untidy ruck ball was cleaned up by the redoubtable Jason Leonard, who barrelled his way forward and presented quick ball to scrum half Dewi Morris a metre into enemy territory.

The number nine then spun possession out to Rob Andrew on the left. England ran a devastating dummy scissors in the midfield with the rampaging Tim Rodber charging in on the reverse angle and drawing in the Welsh centres Nigel Davies and Mike Hall. The space had been created and Andrew fed Phil de Glanville, who in turn hared through the yawning chasm in the defence and over the gain line.

The England centre closed in on the Welsh 22 but full-back Mike Rayer still stood between him and the try line. It was decision time but rather than try and beat his man and risk losing momentum, de Glanville looked for support and it was there in the familiar, fleet-footed form of Underwood speeding up on his inside. The timing of the pass was crucial but the two Englishman were on the same wavelength and just as the tackle inevitably came, de Glanville flicked the ball to the flying wing.

Underwood was clear and accelerated away from the despairing attempt by flanker Mark Perigo to haul him down. Fellow wing Ieuan Evans, however, was still in the hunt but Underwood effortlessly stepped on the gas to leave the Wales skipper clutching thin air and in the blink of an eye he was underneath the posts for England's second try of the match.

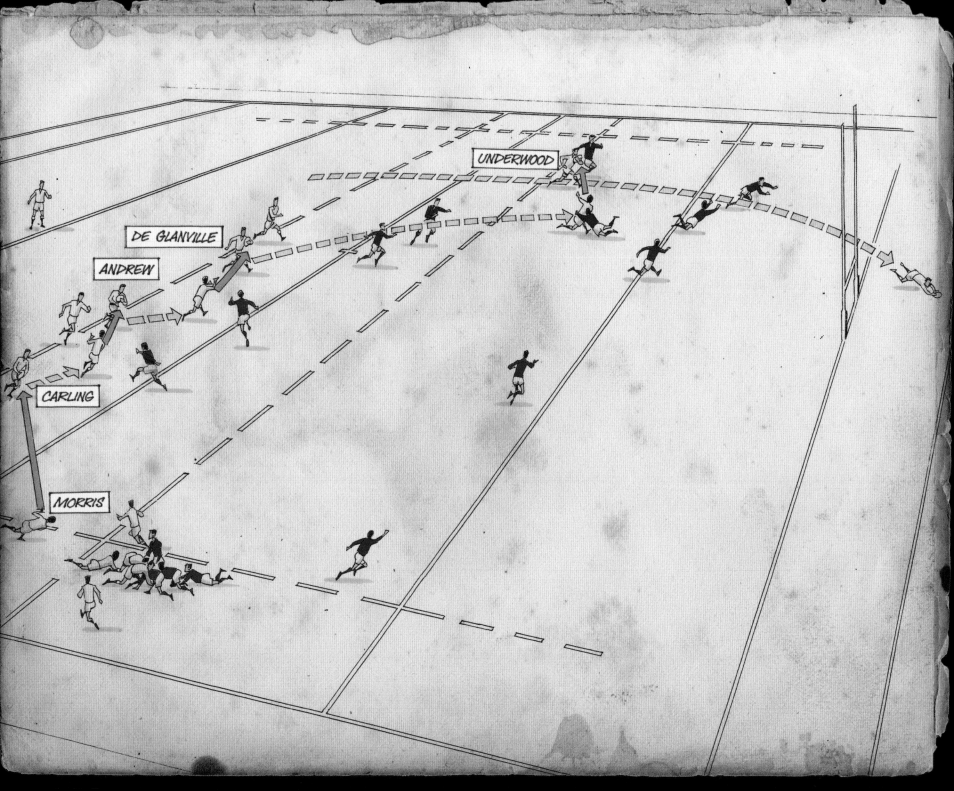

UNDERWOOD

DE GLANVILLE

ANDREW

CARLING

MORRIS

CHRISTOPHE LAMAISON (FRANCE)

V NEW ZEALAND, 31ST OCTOBER 1999

THE 1999 WORLD CUP SEMI-FINAL between Les Bleus and the mighty All Blacks was unquestionably one of the most dramatic in the tournament's history but even by the traditionally high standards of French rugby, Lamaision's try at Twickenham was a masterclass in counter-attacking rugby.

Christophe Lamaison salutes the Twickenham crowd after his breathtaking World Cup semi-final score

It all began with an innocuous New Zealand drop out. Andrew Mehrtens punted the ball deep into the French half and Lamaison, who had only made the starting XV following the withdrawal of the injured Thomas Castaignede, collected possession. As he looked up to survey his options and the advancing Kiwi defenders, it appeared discretion surely had to be the better part of valour.

The French fly half had other ideas and raced forward 15 metres before offloading to Abdel Benazzi. The lock was tackled by Byron Kelleher but France recycled the ball on the half-way line from the resulting ruck and a short pop pass from Fabien Galthie sent Christophe Dominici racing through.

France were now in behind the All Black defence. Dominici beat two New Zealanders inside the 22 as he sped in on the angle from left to right but, just as it seemed the diminutive wing would grab glory for himself, he was spectacularly pulled down by Christian Cullen a metre short of the line.

The French forwards crashed over the ball to keep the move alive and Dominici found himself as the scrum half. He initially looked to go left but realised all the expectant blue shirts lay in the opposite direction and he instantly changed the point of the attack, finding Lamaison to his right with an inch-perfect pass.

The line was at his mercy. The imposing figure of Jonah Lomu was New Zealand's last, forlorn line of defence but with two team-mates lurking outside him, Lamaison held all the cards. Lomu was caught in No Man's Land and the fly half accepted the invitation to stroll over for a stunning try that had an enthralled Twickenham crowd abandoning all thoughts of polite neutrality.

The Kiwis were stunned and although they rallied with two Lomu tries, France were not to be denied a famous victory and three further high-quality scores completed a breathtaking 43-31 triumph that booked Les Bleus place in the World Cup final for a second time.

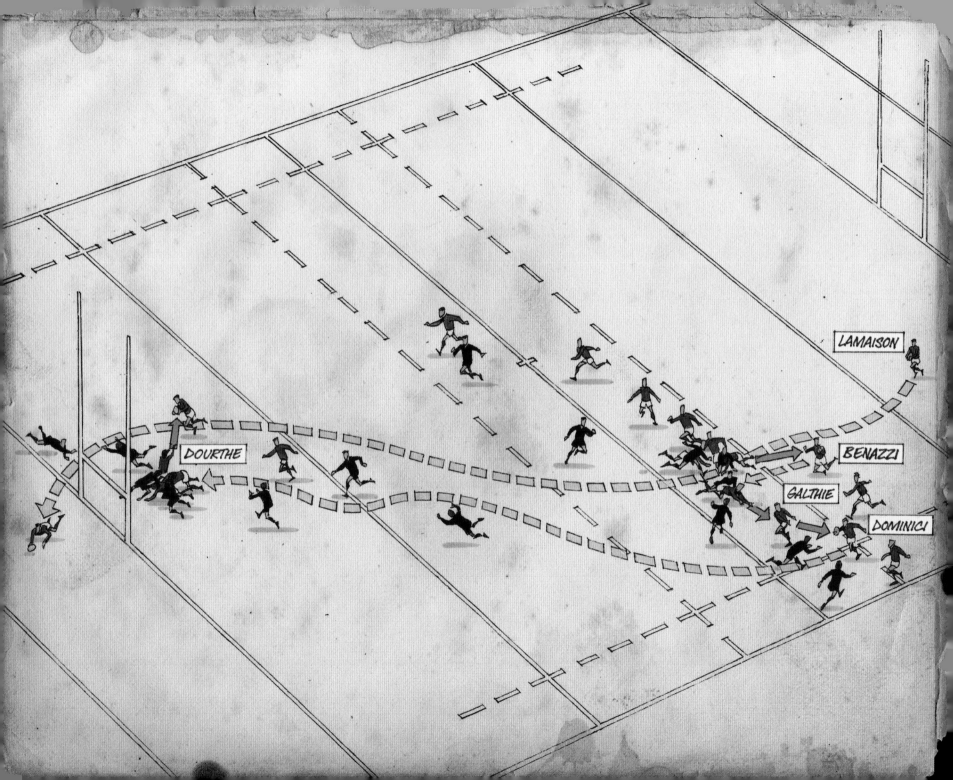

BEN COHEN

V SOUTH AFRICA, NOVEMBER 23RD, 2002

I N HIS INTIMIDATING POMP, Ben Cohen was one of the most destructive and lethal wings the world game has seen and his try in the record-breaking 53-3 demolition of the Springboks was the embodiment of all his pace and power in perfect harmony.

South Africa arrived in London in search of their first victory at Twickenham for five years but England, fresh from victories over the All Blacks and Wallabies on the previous two weekends, were only 12 months away from their crowning glory in the 2003 World Cup and in no mood to accommodate the visitors' burning desire for a triumph in TW1.

Jonny Wilkinson opened the scoring with a 13th minute penalty and a mere eight minutes later Cohen signalled English intent with his superb try.

The move began with an England scrum just outside their 22. Lawrence Dallaglio controlled the ball at the base and, in the blink of an eye, Matt Dawson was away on one of his trademark sniping runs, making huge inroads into the panicked South African ranks.

Butch James shaped to make the tackle but was left wrong-footed by a sublime Dawson step-and-go before he offloaded back to Dallaglio, who in turn fed Mike Tindall. The big centre took the tackle that came crashing in from full-back Werner Greeff and there was Cohen to take the ball on the opposition 22 and provide the cutting edge to a sweeping English attack.

There was still work to do and as Springbok centre Robbie Fleck came rocketing across, the score hung in the balance. Cohen lengthened his stride to get within two metres of the line but Fleck despairingly managed to get hold of his left leg and slow him down.

It was now a power game and Cohen was strong enough to drag his unwanted hitchhiker forward, touching down at the same time as Andre Pretorious flew in a last-ditch attempt to barge him into touch. The try was awarded and Twickenham erupted.

Two minutes later, Springbok second row Jannes Labuschagne was sent off following a cynical late challenge on Wilkinson and England ran riot with six further tries, including a second for Cohen, to send an ominous message to the rest of world game.

Ben Cohen powers accross the line to score against the Springboks in 2002

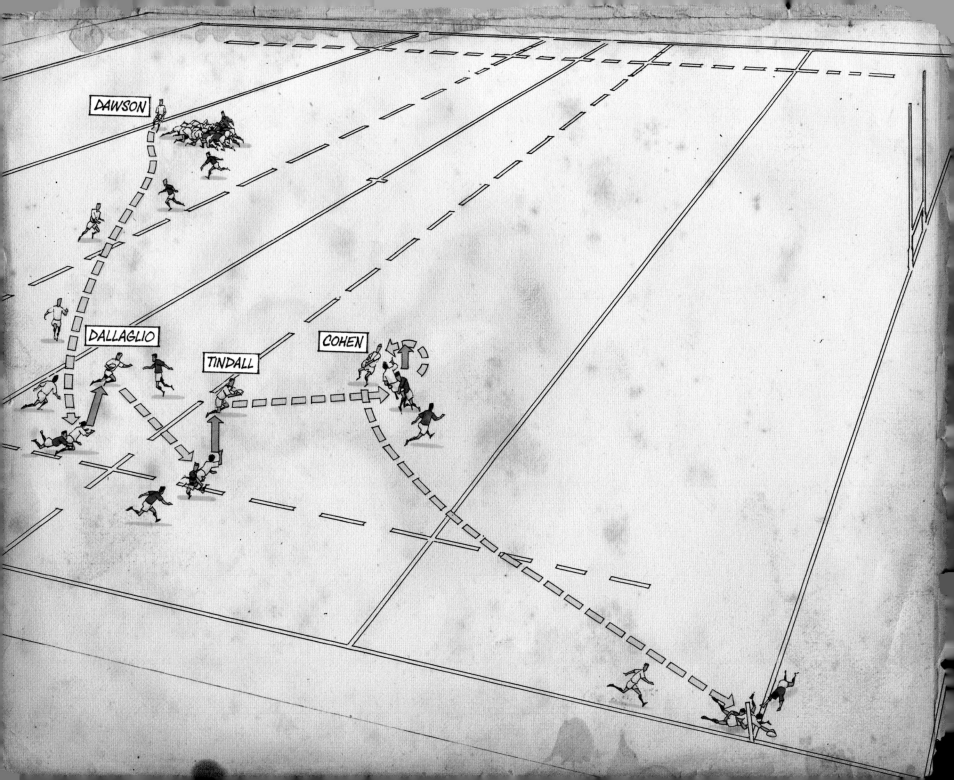

RIKI FLUTEY

V FRANCE, 15TH MARCH 2009

THE 2009 SIX NATIONS CAMPAIGN had been a far from glorious one for English rugby and as Martin Johnson's side prepared to tackle Les Bleus in the wake of narrow defeats to Wales and Ireland, Twickenham was gripped by a pervading sense of trepidation rather than anticipation.

At the end of 80 euphoric minutes, however, the anxiety was forgotten

Riki Flutey crosses the line to score in the 2008 demolition of France

as England celebrated a famous 34-10 rout of their old cross-Channel rivals. Johnson's team scored five tries in the process and the pick of the bunch was undoubtedly their fifth score, a try that ironically had all the hallmarks of a classic French counter-attack.

The second-half at Twickenham was just two minutes old and with England already boasting a commanding 29-0, the emphasis was on the visitors to force the issue. Fly half Francois Trinh-Duc headed into the midfield from a lineout just outside the English 22 but Yannick Jauzion spilled possession in contact and the ball hit the deck.

Andy Goode was the quickest to react, scooping the ball one-handed off the ground and into Flutey's grateful hands and despite being deep in their own half, England immediately sensed the chance to get in behind the French.

Heading left, Flutey passed to Mike Tindall, who in turn moved the ball to Delon Armitage. The defence was coming across in waves but the turbo-charged full-back was in full, majestic flow and he left both Mathieu Bastareaud and Sebastien Chabal trailing ignominiously in his slipstream as he raced over the halfway line and towards the try line.

Full-back Maxime Medard however was still minding the French shop and Armitage selflessly looked for support, throwing a looping pass infield from left to right and there was Flutey, displaying impeccable timing, to take the ball.

The burning question was whether the centre had the pace to round off the move and with French wing Cedric Heymans in hot pursuit, the crowd held their breath. Flutey got to within two metres when Heymans pounced. He failed to make a clean tackle but the contact sent Flutey tumbling, followed by an untidy forward roll but he got to his feet and, just as Julien Malzieu arrived, he dived triumphantly over the line.

There were no further England tries in the game but the memory of Flutey's roof-raising effort ensured the Twickenham faithful streamed out of the stadium after the final whistle with their spirits raised and pre-match fears dispelled.

GOODE

FLUTEY

TINDALL

ARMITAGE

All Blacks magic leaves England clinging on

The Sunday Telegraph

Sunday, 10th November 2002

By Paul Ackford

My God, they are worth the wait. New Zealand may travel infrequently but when they do they are pure box office. This was a sensational Test match, haunted by the giant Jonah Lomu, full of dramatic changes in fortune and a game in which England were anxiously hanging in there at the death.

When the final whistle brought this wonderful afternoon to an end it was the arms of the England players which were raised aloft and if there was an edge of sheepishness in that gesture, it was understandable. Had Ben Cohen not scythed down Ben Blair close to the corner flag two minutes from time, then the All Blacks would have confounded pundits and posted a dramatic victory.

For England to work so hard to see them off is an indication of just how good New Zealand will be in the World Cup, and just how hard England will have to fight to justify the favourable billing they will undoubtedly take into that tournament.

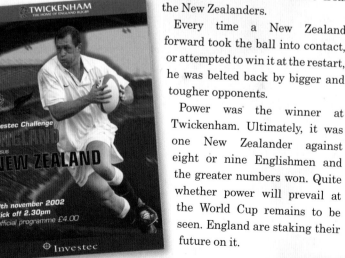

England coach Clive Woodward might get fed up with everyone banging on about this World Cup but, in essence, yesterday's encounter with the All Blacks was all about that great competition. The two sides treated Twickenham to an insight into their respective philosophies.

England's was simple. They base their game on size and power. Forwards like Phil Vickery, Trevor Woodman, Martin Johnson, Lewis Moody and Danny Grewcock are all about bulk and power going forward. They have a licence to roam and hooker Steve Thompson is their spiritual and physical leader. Thompson was sensational yesterday. He and his burly mates smashed into the Blacks and tore great chunks of resolve from the New Zealanders.

Every time a New Zealand forward took the ball into contact, or attempted to win it at the restart, he was belted back by bigger and tougher opponents.

Power was the winner at Twickenham. Ultimately, it was one New Zealander against eight or nine Englishmen and the greater numbers won. Quite whether power will prevail at the World Cup remains to be seen. England are staking their future on it.

Cohen and Wilkinson save the citadel

Independent on Sunday

Sunday, 17th November 2002

By Tim Glover

It's getting better week by week. In a game of swings and roundabouts, with a rollercoaster and a big dipper thrown in, England completed their first hat-trick of victories over Australia on another bewitching afternoon at headquarters. It did not seem possible to surpass last week's engrossing match in which the All Blacks were defeated here 31-28, but somehow they managed it.

At the end the stadium, not for the first time, was filled with the theme tune from The Great Escape – echoing the manner of England's extraordinary rise, fall and rise before getting home by two goals and six penalties to two goals, a try and four penalties.

The reason, once again, was the golden boot of Jonny Wilkinson. Yesterday he gave another world-class exhibition of goal-kicking, contributing 22 points: six out of six penalties – whatever the distance it

made no difference – and he converted both England's tries.

Matt Burke is no amateur in this department but, crucially, he failed with a penalty in the second minute, another in the 76th and missed a conversion as the world champions scored three tries to two. Their tries all came in the space of seven minutes, during which Australia scored 19 points, completely transforming the complexion of a match that England seemed to have under lock and key.

Leading 16-6, which did not reflect the run of play – the margin should have been greater – England were hit by a blitz from the Wallabies and suddenly found themselves trailing 16-25. After 55 minutes, it was 19-31. To their immense credit England, having apparently lost the plot, did not forget the punchline. Wilkinson's penalties chipped away at Australia's lead, setting up a stunning climax.

They were still six points adrift in the final quarter when James Simpson-Daniel, sadly neglected for the most part on the right wing, appeared in midfield and slipped a sublime pass to Ben Cohen, who had the momentum, the pace and the angle to cross for his second try. It was his 18th in 20 Tests, a tremendous strike rate. Wilkinson's conversion, of course, was a formality but it was the kick that gave his side their one-point victory.

MATCHDAY AT HQ

A MASSIVE TEAM EFFORT

THE SIGHT OF TWICKENHAM on an international match day, groaning contentedly at the seams with 82,000 boisterous but good-natured supporters, is one which those fortunate enough to have witnessed first hand will never forget.

The stadium springs into life in the hours leading up to an eagerly-anticipated kick-off but, like the proverbial duck gliding gracefully on the water whilst paddling like crazy below the surface, Twickenham is a hive of frenetic activity behind-the-scenes on matchday to ensure everything from the catering to the post-match player interviews run as smoothly as possible.

It takes an army of stewards – whose ranks always include a vicar, a gynaecologist and undertaker so that all potential matters of life and death are prepared for – chefs and bar staff to make HQ tick as the fans descend on the ground and there are hours of preparation before the referee finally blows his whistle to get the action started.

The first priority on the morning of the game is to undertake a security sweep of the stadium. Some 1,000 gatemen and stewards, 400 of them honorary, will be on duty for the match itself but before they can take up their positions the ground is thoroughly searched before the public is allowed in.

Nigel Cox – RFU Operations Manager & Matchday Safety Officer

"My main role on a matchday is to oversee all issues relating to security and safety, which essentially means liaising with the police, local council, the relevant RFU staff and the 400 honorary Twickenham stewards who are in attendance for an international game.

"I arrive at the ground at around 6.30 on the morning of the match and my first job is to oversee a complete search of the ground. We're obviously looking for anything suspicious that shouldn't be there, but it's also to ensure that fire exits aren't blocked and stairways are clear.

"At some time between 10 and 12 I will escort two representatives from Richmond Council, who award the day's safety certificate. Technically they could stop the crowd coming in if they aren't happy with something but, fingers crossed, we've never had that problem.

"The outer gates open at 11 and that's when things start getting hectic as the fans pour in. We've got 80 cameras around the ground to monitor the flow of people all the way back to Richmond and we're always checking to see particular gates aren't getting too busy.

"I tend to spend the match in the control room in the north-west corner of the ground, which is where the representatives of the police, fire and ambulance services are also based, monitoring the crowd. I'm looking for people who may need help and sadly one of the main problems is supporters having heart attacks, which is why we have defibrillators dotted all over the place.

"Once the final whistle goes, my priority is to get everyone safely out of the stadium and on their journeys home. The bars close two-and-a-half hours after the end of the game, so all being well I knock off at about eight in the evening."

Top left: The crowds start to gather outside the new South Stand

Top right: Corporate guests tuck into their pre-match meal

Bottom left: The famous pre-match scene in the West car park

Bottom right: Pre-match at the Rugby Store

Richard Knight – Twickenham Stadium Director

"I get to Twickenham at around 8.30 in the morning and my role is to oversee the ground's operations, which includes everything from security to issues with the bars and catering. If things run smoothly, I tend not to get too involved.

"I've basically got a roving brief. I will wander around the stadium as the supporters come in and act as the eyes and ears for the various departments. I'm always clutching a radio so people can get in touch and I'm looking out for queues at one of the bars or congestion on the stairs, so I can alert the relevant people and get it sorted.

"The RFU has a legal responsibility for the stadium and the car parks that surround the stadium. Once they are empty after the game, I can hand over to the security staff to physically lock the ground up.

"Since the Twickenham capacity has increased following the completion of the South Stand, we've coped well with the challenge of looking after 7,000 extra supporters but the official opening in 2006 was almost a nightmare.

"We had sold all the 82,000 tickets but an hour-and-a-half before kick-off the builders were still drilling the holes to fix the last seats down, which was the most nerve-wracking moment I've had in my eight years working for the RFU."

MATCHDAY TIMELINE

6.00am: Staff offices and event control room open

6.30am: First security checks undertaken

6.45am: Kitchens open and food preparation begins

8.30am: Chief Steward's briefing

9.30am: Rugby House reception opens

11.00am: Richmond Council officers inspect the ground before issuing safety certificate.

11.00am: Ticket Office opens

11.00am: Outer gates open to the public

11.00am: World Rugby Museum opens

11.30am: West Car Park bar opens

11.30am: Rugby Store opens

12.30pm: Level Two bars open

1.15pm: Match officials arrive at HQ

1.30pm: England team bus arrives at Gate B, West Car Park

1.30pm: Gates to seating areas open

1.35pm: Opposition team bus arrives

2.30pm: Players' pre-match warm-up

2.30pm: Pre-match entertainment begins

3.00pm: Kick-off

4.30pm: Final whistle

7.00pm: Bars close

8.30pm: Post-match players' dinner in the Spirit of Rugby Restaurant begins

10.00pm: Kitchens close

11.00pm: Stadium locked up

ELSEWHERE IN THE STADIUM, up to 30 separate kitchens are fired up in readiness for the massive catering and corporate hospitality operation that goes on, largely unseen, on a matchday.

Twickenham boasts 155 corporate boxes and there are a further 15 restaurants located in the stands. For any given big game, up to 10,500 meals will be served throughout the day courtesy of the 2,500 kitchen staff employed for the occasion.

The ground's biggest restaurant is the Rose Suite in the South Stand, which can seat 800. Some 250 can be accommodated in Obolensky's in the East Stand while the more intimate atmosphere of the unique Twickenham Cellar beneath the West Stand caters for just 14 discerning diners (see *Behind The Scenes*).

Seating up to 650 people, the Spirit of Rugby Restaurant is Twickenham's second largest dining area and, for those with a romantic rugby bent, it is licensed to host civil weddings. In recent years it has also been the venue for the official post-match dinner attended by players, officials and guests.

Two of the thousands of meals served on every internatiuonal matchday

Ryan Matthee – RFU Head Chef

"On average we will serve around 8,000 sit-down meals at the ground on matchday, although it can be as many as 10,500 so you can imagine there is an incredible amount of preparation that goes into the catering operation and a lot of staff involved.

"The menus are all planned weeks before the big day, which I sometimes try and theme around the nationality of the opposition, and the food preparation will begin on the Tuesday before the weekend. I will brief my 30 leading chefs on the day before the game and I'll arrive at Twickenham on matchday at around five in the morning.

"In total, there'll be roughly 100 chefs working on the day and four to five other extra people in each kitchen. We can have up to 30 kitchens running for an international.

"I don't do any cooking on matchday. My job is to go around the kitchens and ensure that the food going out meets our standards of quality and consistency and no-one is having problems with their fridges or gas supply.

"We serve the first meals at 1pm and we also cater for the post-match players' dinner which is held on Six Nations days and after the autumn internationals in the Spirit of Rugby restaurant and is attended by the teams, wives and girlfriends and officials. That starts at 8.30 and if there are no problems, I'll knock off at around 9.30 once the food has been served.

"It is a massive challenge catering at Twickenham because of the sheer size of the place but the atmosphere is incredible on a matchday and there's a huge sense of satisfaction when the last plate is sent out and everything has gone smoothly."

RUGBY FANS OF COURSE ARE notoriously thirsty creatures and there are a grand total of 26 bars inside the stadium, plus temporary hostelries in the West Car Park, to ensure everyone can get a drink. The longest of them all, the Scrum Bar, is to be found in the north-east corner of the ground. At 47.5 metres it is the longest bar at any sporting venue in Britain, boasts 96 pumps and up to 44 very, very busy staff.

The Scrum Bar serves around 6,000 pints on matchday and in total up to 90,000 will be gratefully consumed by parched supporters before, during and up to two-and-a-half hours after the match. To complement the many watering holes, Twickenham has nine fixed fast food stalls and 29 extra mobile units in operation on a match day.

Fans eager for a souvenir of their big day spend around £220,000 at the Twickenham Rugby Store on the day of a big game while the 50 programmes sellers on duty will sell some 30,000 copies during the day.

With the supporters fed, watered and safely into the stadium, attention turns to the rugby. The England team arrive by coach from their base in Bagshot an-hour-and-a-half before kick-off and they disappear into the home changing room in the West Stand, where their kit and final pre-match rituals await them. Team manager Martin Johnson will conduct his pre-match interviews for an expectant media and after the national anthems, battle finally commences.

After the match, the focus swiftly switches to getting the fans home in an orderly fashion. An estimated 35,000 of the 82,000-strong crowd make their way on foot to Twickenham mainline station and other local tube and mainline stations while at least 6,000 use the bus shuttle service that runs between the ground and Richmond.

Around three hours after the final whistle, the stadium is virtually deserted. The supporters have evaporated into the early evening and the public bars and food outlets are shut. The players may remain for the traditional post-match dinner and speeches but otherwise Twickenham is largely silent after another frantic and fascinating day of international rugby.

Richard Prescott – England Teams Media Director

"The media accreditation has always been taken care of before the match, so I will get to the stadium at around 10. My first job is to review the morning's press coverage in the newspapers so I can flag up any issues to Martin Johnson that could come up in his pre and post-match interview sessions.

"I'll then check everything is in order in the press box in the East Stand, the photographers' room in the North and the commentary gantry in the West to make sure there are no technical issues or problems.

"At midday I will talk to the floor manager from the host broadcaster to see if they have any special requests on the day and to ensure their cameras and equipment are not obstructing the fans' view anywhere in the ground.

"The team buses arrive around an hour-and-half before kick-off and it's my job to alert the broadcaster, whether it's Sky or the BBC, that they're here so they can get a shot of the players.

"I watch the match from the mouth of the players' tunnel. It's not the best view in the house but means I'm close to everything that's going on. I keep a note of the key moments and incidents so I can brief the coaching team before all the post-match media work.

"I'll sit down with Martin and the guys for five minutes after the match, so everyone can catch their breath before facing the media. Win or lose, it's important to let the adrenaline die down before talking to the press.

"The players and the coaches are finished with the media two hours after the final whistle, which then gives me the chance to get a match report up on the RFU website. After that, I'm pretty much done and I'll head home at around eight."

The party continues long after the match, especially if England have won!

Dave Tennison – RFU Equipment Co-ordinator

"Essentially I'm the England team's kit man on matchdays. I arrive at Twickenham at nine in the morning for a three o'clock kick-off and I aim to have all the kit, equipment and extras laid out and organised in the changing room by 11.30.

"Each player gets two shirts and two pairs of shorts, plus one pair of socks for a game and it's my job to ensure everyone gets the right sizes. Our official kit supplier is Nike but we get the shirts delivered by a logistics firm called FXMS in Basingstoke, who do the embroidery with the players' names, the game and the date, on Friday afternoon.

"I keep the shirts in a storeroom by the side of the players' entrance and transfer them and things like clean towels and tackle shields into the changing room. I also lay out match programmes, soap, shampoo, bottles of water and Powerade.

"It's important the players don't have to worry about things like kit, studs or whatever so I'm on hand if they've got any special requests like blacking out logos on scrum caps or gloves while someone like Phil Vickery likes a black coffee before a game.

"The match itself is my quietest time during the day. I head back to the changing room five minutes before half-time to tidy up and ensure there are no ice packs on the floor that the players can slip on. I stay in the background when the coach gives his half-time team talk but I'm always on hand if any of the squad need something.

"It's carnage after full time when the team come in and throw everything around. There's tackle shields, water bottles, scrum caps – anything you can think of – strewn all over the floor but I let the players get showered and changed before attempting to tidy up. There's no laundry to be done because the players keep all their kit as souvenirs or to give to family or charity."

England inflict pain on brutal bully boys

The Sunday Times

Sunday, 24th November 2002

By Stephen Jones

England smashed South Africa into pieces, inflicting on them easily the biggest defeat the Springboks have suffered, and rounding off a brilliant autumn in which they have convincingly put away all the three southern hemisphere rugby giants, and in which the whole sport in the country grew with them.

There is no room for carping or devaluing. Not only with their results but with their courage, ambition and entertainment value, they have been superb. Yesterday they scored seven tries and were able to absorb the loss of Jonny Wilkinson, who was put out of the game by one of a torrent of illegal challenges. But Austin Healey merely trotted on, marked his 50th cap by showing real sharpness as replacement fly-half, while a motley combination of Matt Dawson, Tim Stimpson and Andy Gomarsall rubbed it in by sending over immaculate conversions.

Furthermore, England's forwards drove the life out of South Africa with notable performances from Phil Vickery, Neil Back and Lawrence Dallaglio. The team now sits at the summit of their own rugby history, and English rugby has never been so well-served, in achievement and spirit, by its national team.

The fact that Jannes Labuschagne, the South African lock, was sent off after 22 minutes must not detract from this performance. England were well in charge before he left, with the South African scrum in constant trouble in the first quarter. In fact, South Africa were clueless as to whether they had a full complement or not.

It was particularly satisfying to see the Springbok forwards shattered by driving mauls, to see Fleck hammered by a thunderous tackle by Steve Thompson, then bouncing off the charging Vickery; and to see a shattering pushover try by the England pack, which ran the score up to the 50-point mark.

England commendably kept their focus in the second half. Greenwood finished off a sweeping move with real elan by scoring down the left wing. England cut them to pieces again and Phil Christophers was sent careering down the right-hand touchline. Full-back Werner Greeff came across and caught Christophers round the neck with a swinging arm a few yards from the line. The incident fulfilled every last one of the criteria for a penalty try and the referee made the correct call.

Healey was now beavering away as England went for the half-century and Dallaglio touched down the final pushover try, which was nothing more than England deserved. And precisely what South Africa deserved.

Sheridan and his power pack force a change to rule book

GREAT MATCHES

ENGLAND 26 AUSTRALIA 16

Saturday, 12th November 2005

The Guardian

Monday, 14th November 2005

By Robert Kitson

Nothing so far has withstood the black juggernaut thundering through Britain and Ireland but New Zealand will collide with a much sterner force of nature this weekend. No Wallabies front row has ever been splattered across the windshield to such gruesome effect and England, if nothing else, have unearthed a weapon capable of stopping even the world's best in their tracks.

The first thing to say about Andrew Sheridan's contribution to a power-laden home win was that, thankfully, no one was paralysed. Scans on the Australian prop Matt Dunning, to everyone's relief, revealed no serious neck injury, although the damage to the psyche of Sheridan's other hapless stooge Al Baxter may prove permanent. Not since William 'The Refrigerator' Perry rumbled over the NFL horizon has a tight forward made such an awesome close-quarters impression.

A possible consequence is that the 26-year-old Sale prop, along with his fellow giants in the English pack, will force the International Rugby Board to tweak the laws of the game. When Dunning went down in a worrying heap within a minute of Baxter being sin-binned for yet again failing to stay upright, it left the French referee Joel Jutge no option but to order uncontested scrums at a time when Australia were being corkscrewed into oblivion.

At a stroke England's strength effectively became a weakness and, without a 75th-minute try from Mark Cueto, they might conceivably have lost. No wonder Andy Robinson, England's head coach, is suggesting the IRB undertakes an urgent review of the rules governing front-row replacements.

Given this was Sheridan's first start for his country – as opposed to Baxter's 29th – and he has only played prop for three years, it was even more impressive. How ironic, having told everyone how England need to expand their game to retain the World Cup, if Robinson ends up with a identikit version of the 2003 side who kept it tight better than anyone else.

At times England's forward dominance bordered on the farcical; Corry messed up one potential pushover simply because the Wallabies scrum was careering backwards too fast. Against all odds the promising Drew Mitchell was driven over and Mat Rogers converted to level the scores at 16-16 with 25 minutes to go. In the end Harry Houdini was not clad in green and gold but the Wallabies displayed considerable guts; barely five minutes remained when Cueto, following 17 phases, applied the killer blow.

THE FANS

Intrepid fans risk life and limb to catch a glimpse of England's 1929 match with Wales

SACRED GROUND

IF TWICKENHAM IS A MODERN CATHEDRAL OF RUGBY, then it is nothing without its faithful worshippers and the millions of devout, if not exactly abstemious fans who have poured through the turnstiles since that first international game between England and Wales in 1910. The fans have, of course, played an integral part in the history and the heritage of the famous old ground.

The exact number of supporters who have cheered England on over the years is lost in the midst of time but as the decades have come and gone their numbers have inexorably swelled. Some 18,000 were on hand to watch England's inaugural win over the Welsh but just three years later a crowd of 29,000 filled HQ for the visit of the touring Springboks and by the 1950s the stadium was regularly attracting 75,000 fans for England games. Today, 82,000 come to worship whenever the men in white are in action.

Avid supporter King George V gave Twickenham the royal seal of approval

when he attended the first post-War match in TW1 in 1919 but it has been the legions of ordinary fans through the eras who have collectively transformed the mere bricks and mortar of Twickenham into the spiritual home of English rugby.

In 1930 it was clearly not done to leave for the rugby without your hat

ENGLAND | **EAST STAND**

NEW ZEALANDERS
At TWICKENHAM
Saturday, 3rd Jan., 1925
Kick off 2.30 p.m.

Block W

NOTE: Entrance to Ground in Whitton Road
Entrance to Seats at BACK of Stand.

Row 20 Seat 755

Price - 10/-

St. Cooper.

ENGLAND
v
WALES
At TWICKENHAM
Saturday, Jan. 20th, 1923
Kick off 2.45 p.m.

Price 7/6
(including Admission to Ground and
Amusement Tax if purchased before the day)

RING SEATS

West Side
ENTRANCE in WHITTON ROAD

Section 3

Row 4 Seat 146

C. J. B. Marriott
Secretary R.U.

N.B.—OFFICIAL PROGRAMMES can be purchased INSIDE the Gates ONLY

The crowd overflowed onto
the edge of the pitch at
the England v Wales
match in 1935

HIGH JINX AT HQ

BONHOMIE AND CAMARADERIE are the hallmarks of matchday, but not all have always been quite so impeccably behaved. The suited and booted crowd at the Middlesex Sevens in 1929 invaded the pitch in

between fixtures for an impromptu game while the students who watched the 1965 Varsity Match surreptitiously helped themselves to a crossbar from one end of the ground after the final whistle.

In the early days it became traditional for Welsh fans, more often than not accompanied by giant home-grown leeks, to invade the pitch before or after the match and scale the posts. More recently the supporters at the 1994 Middlesex Sevens nearly tore the old West Stand down by hand after the final in the search for souvenirs, spurred on by the knowledge that it was scheduled for demolition just a few days later.

High jinx indeed but the two most famous exponents of outrageous behaviour at HQ have to be Michael O'Brien and Erica Roe in the 70s and 80s and their famous streaks on the hallowed turf, much to the amusement of the thronged stands (*See Magic Moments*).

Far left: How any of the 1932 Varsity Match crowd found their way back to the right car is a mystery

Left, top: An impromptu game breaks out between matches at the 1929 Middlesex Sevens

Left, middle and bottom: The crowd at England v Scotland, 1932

Inset: Armed with a prize leek, a Welsh fan scales the Twickenham posts in 1932

Chris Oti's 1988 hat-trick struck a chord with England fans

SWING LOW, SWEET CHARIOT

A SEMINAL MOMENT IN HQ'S HISTORY came in 1988 with the visit of Ireland in the Five Nations. England were on a dismal run of form and at half-time they trailed 3-0 as Twickenham echoed to the sounds of 'Molly Malone' sung by the travelling Irish support.

It was however to be the proverbial game of two halves and after the break England exploded into life, inspired by a hat-trick from wing Chris Oti. At some unidentified point, sections of the crowd began singing the gospel hymn turned rugby song 'Swing Low, Swing Chariot' as England stormed to a famous 35-3 triumph.

No-one knew it at the time but Twickenham had just adopted its unofficial anthem and totemic rallying cry.

HQ MEMORIES

Lawrence Dallaglio

"One of my great memories of Twickenham is actually as a fan not a player. It was back in the days of the old Twickenham. It was 1991 and the Grand Slam decider between England and France. It was the match that had the try when Philippe Saint-Andre scored at the end of a move which had begun under the France posts.

"I was in the West Stand with the rest of the England Under-19 team. We had just played the Italy Under-19 team in Cambridge and had been given tickets for the match. We were down near the touchline in our blazers and the noise was unbelievable.

"Twickenham is a magnificent stadium now, but it was still very impressive then. I remember Brian Moore, the England hooker, coming over to take a line-out right in front of us and he had to ask what the lineout call was a few times before he got it. The atmosphere was incredible that day."

THERE'S SOMETHING ABOUT MARY

MARY TOOTELL – REGULAR AT TWICKENHAM FOR 50 YEARS

"THE FIRST TIME I WENT TO TWICKENHAM was back in 1949 for the Calcutta Cup game against Scotland. I was serving with the Women's Royal Air Force in Gloucester and a chap who was winning his first cap gave me a couple of tickets. I think he had a thing for girls in uniforms.

"I was born in Ireland and was a member of the Cork Constitution club at the age of four but I came to England when I was 18 and I've supported them ever since. The rest of the family still won't speak to me.

"I started standing at the entrance of the players' tunnel 26 years ago. My husband had died not long before and I thought it was time to get as close as I could so I threw myself at lots of fit, young men. It makes me feel young.

"I always give the England captain a red rose and a card. My favourite captain was Will Carling and his late mother once told me he had kept every single card I'd given him. I wanted to take him home with me and keep him safe from all those women.

"The messages are just silly little messages of encouragement. I gave Steve Borthwick a card with a dog lying on a deckchair before the Australia game a couple of years ago. The message read, "I do not want to see any of you boys lying down like this waiting for a big Aussie to jump on you."

"I remember at one game I was standing at the players' entrance and I

caught Bill Beaumont out of the corner of my eye coming towards me. He was carrying a huge bouquet of flowers which he said were in recognition of all my support. I told him I didn't want recognition, I just wanted them to win.

"Bill once asked me to go and visit Tony Bond in hospital. Tony had broken his leg in the Ireland match and Bill thought he'd appreciate a visit, so I went to see him at Middlesex Hospital on the Monday and the Irish ward sister told me I could talk to him as he came out of the anaesthetic. He was still sedated because he'd broken his leg again when he'd come around the first time and heard an Irish accent. It must have been the shock and when I saw him they'd tied the leg to the side of the bed to stop him doing himself another mischief.

"I've had so many great moments at Twickenham but I think my favourite sight was watching Rory Underwood tearing down the wing and scoring a try.

"I'm in my 80s now and when I finally go I want my ashes to be fed into the middle of a scrum when England play Wales. Being allowed to get so close to the players makes me feel part of it and I want my final resting place to be on the pitch."

TWICKENHAM'S MR ENGLAND

PETER CROSS – THE OFFICIAL ENGLAND TEAM MASCOT

"THE FIRST TIME I DRESSED UP FOR A SPORTING EVENT was the Olympics in Atlanta in 1996. It had been a lifetime ambition to go to a major sporting event like that and I decided to mark the occasion with a special outfit. It was a Union Jack Arab outfit and when I got back from America I thought I'd try it out at Twickenham for the game against Argentina in November.

"I had a Union Jack suit made for the Lions tour to South Africa in 1997 but after a few comments, I decided to get a St George's Cross suit for Twickenham because it was more appropriate for England games. A good friend of my sister's called Eileen made it for me and I've got three now in case of emergencies.

"The RFU called me in 2000 to ask whether I wanted to become the team's official mascot. I came up to Twickenham to talk it over and once I'd convinced the security officer I was the right sort of chap, they offered me the job. I don't get paid but it's a huge privilege to be the England mascot.

"The atmosphere at Twickenham is always electric. The buzz I get walking around the pitch before kick-off, interacting with the crowd, is amazing but the highlight for me is standing opposite the teams when they sing the national anthems. It's pure, raw emotion and it never fails to make the hairs on the back of my neck stand up.

"People always want to have their picture taken with me. More often than not it's the visiting fans who ask me to pose and it's a part of the role I love. Rugby fans are the best in the world and the fact there's no segregation or problems speaks volumes about the game.

"My favourite Twickenham moment has to be the game against Australia in 2000. It was my first match as the official mascot and it was a cracking game which we won with a late Dan Luger try. It was the start of a golden era for England during which we regularly beat the southern hemisphere sides and I'll never forget Sir Clive Woodward taking me into the changing room to meet the players.

"I have to admit I was a little worried when they were building the new South Stand and whether it would affect the atmosphere but if anything it's even better now."

Peter Cross has been the England mascot at Twickenham since 2000

Princes Harry and William are regulars in the Twickenham crowd

That's one hell of a pasty! The Cornish invasion of 1999

The Middlesex Sevens is just one big fancy dress party in certain circles

FAN-TASTIC

TODAY, HQ REMAINS A PLACE OF PILGRIMAGE FOR England fans and opposition supporters who invariably bring a burst of colour to the stadium as they proudly sport national emblems in support of their team.

Leeks abound when Wales are in town while cockerels are de rigeur when France play. But other than a spot of poultry crowd control or apprehending errant streakers, the police on duty at the ground are rarely called into action.

"Thankfully rowdy behaviour is really not a big problem," says Nigel Cox, the RFU's Operations Manager & Matchday Safety Officer. "On average we have to eject perhaps two or three people from a crowd of 82,000 on an international day.

"The culture of the game is to have a few beers and a laugh with the opposition supporters. Occasionally somebody has one too many but that's as serious as it gets. Our main focus is overall crowd safety rather than having to deal with trouble makers."

Fancy dress, face paint and casually-dressed heirs to the throne are all familiar sights at the stadium in the modern era. Not quite what King George was accustomed to in his day but just as HQ has changed physically over the years, so too have the men, women and children who continue to be as much part of the Twickenham experience as what happens on the pitch.

Cipriani banishes England blues

The Daily Telegraph
Monday, 17th March 2008
By Mick Cleary

The shaping of a new era has proved a troublesome pursuit for Brian Ashton but, at last, he seems to have alighted on one man who might just turn those feint marks on the canvas into something of lasting value.

Danny Cipriani's brush strokes were vivid and colourful, lighting up an overcast Twickenham afternoon. They stood in stark contrast to the monochrome version of England imprinted on the minds of the spectators, the opening salvo against Wales and the staunch display in Paris notwithstanding. From being dull and leaden, England were sprightly and potent.

But if Cipriani could do this on closing weekend, then why wasn't he set free to do it from the start? Those questions continue to swirl around Ashton, who has quelled but not wholly dismissed speculation about his own future as England coach.

England handed over the early initiative to Ireland in much the manner they had against Scotland seven days earlier. They ceded position and possession from where Ireland swept over for a converted try from Rob Kearney and a penalty from Ronan O'Gara.

That England did not panic faced with a 10-0 deficit, with its Groundhog overtones, is to their credit. Cipriani led the way on that front, controlling the tempo and challenging those around him,

and in front of him. How refreshing too, to see a bloke kick a ball 50 to 60 metres rather than the piddly, safety-first options.

Jamie Noon ought to have teed up a score for his support runners after being worked through a hole by his own good efforts as well as those of Cipriani in the 225th minute. England were already on the move by that point, Paul Sackey rounding off a sequence that he had begun himself and which was sustained by good work from flanker Michael Lipman.

Lesley Vainikolo had a hand in two of England's three tries, sweeping in as the extra man for Mathew Tait's 57th minute score, and coming through on a decoy run for Jamie noon's try ten minutes from time.

Ireland were cast adrift. O'Gara, captain for the day, was woefully out of sorts. So, also, were too many of his team-mates.

England know the feeling. For now, at least, Cipriani has emphatically banished those blues.

JONNO'S TROOPS COME ALIVE WITH FIVE-TRY ROUT

Daily Mail

Monday, 16th March 2009

By Peter Jackson

Just when even the most one-eyed among the Red Rose legion feared an imminent deepening of the depression which had been hanging over HQ for five years, the tournament's champion under-performers pre-empted another crisis in a style beyond their wildest dreams.

Five tries, all done and dusted as early as the 42nd minute, added up to the most startling result of the championship. A team who had spent every one of their six previous Tests hurtling down the global rankings like Franz Klammer on the piste, went out knowing that one more failure would be one too many, that one more yellow card would invite further ridicule and that another defeat would put their besieged captain in the line of renewed fire.

The spectre of finishing the tournament in a dishonourable dispute over fifth place with Scotland on Saturday would have done nothing for Steve Borthwick's credibility, nor Martin Johnson's. France, fresh from their ambush of Wales in Paris 16 days earlier, arrived espousing hatred for their neighbours and claiming they were ready for a war.

In the event, it was all over after barely a minute. To be precise, this will go down as the 69-second war – the time it took Riki Flutey's bewitching feet to send a star called Mark Cueto thundering down the home straight.

Suddenly, Johnson had leapt out of his seat above the tunnel, his raised fist telling a very different story from Croke Park a fortnight ago when he used it in anger at the stupidity of Danny Care's sin-binning. This time, England's manager used his big right hand to acknowledge the sheer verve of surely the fastest try the old tournament has witnessed since John Leslie's touchdown ten seconds into Scotland's home match against Wales ten years ago.

On a day when English hospitality extended to making the visitors feel at home in positively Mediterranean conditions, not even old beetlebrows could have dreamt that he would end up watching a rout.

And so it came to pass, an England team free of the shackles at last unleashed a flood of invention rarely seen since the days when Johnson was out there at the helm.

BEYOND RUGBY

Horses grazed on the Twickenham turf during World War I, before being sent to the front

WORLD WAR I

ALTHOUGH TWICKENHAM WILL ALWAYS BE SYNONYMOUS with the drama and bone-crunching cut and thrust of both international and top-class rugby, the grand old stadium has not always been the exclusive preserve of 30 muscular men, two sets of posts and one odd-shaped ball.

In fact, the ground had enjoyed a mere five seasons of Test match rugby before the outbreak of war in 1914 forced the RFU to mothball the stadium until the end of hostilities. The old East and West Stands lay dormant during the conflict but the pitch was used for grazing horses before they were sent to the distinctly more turbulent surroundings of the Western Front.

After the War, as life returned to some sort of normality and rugby returned to Twickenham, there were occasions when the pitch was used for what can only be loosely termed 'rugby', or even 'sport'.

Spontaneous games of rugby involving hundreds of enthusiastic suited and booted supporters soon became a traditional pastime between matches at the Middlesex Sevens tournament after the first event in 1926.

The unusual picture on this page, middle right, with the crowd on the pitch playing some sort of game with an enormous inflatable ball, is believed to have been taken in 1927, possibly at the Middlesex Sevens.

The occasion of the sack race, or game of sack rugby, is also not known for certain. However, the protaganists do appear to be wearing rugby shirts so perhaps this event was also part of the fun and games at the Sevens one year.

Spontaneous, hundreds-a-side 'rugby' games would break out between matches in the early days of the Middlesex Sevens

A giant inflatable ball amuses the Twickenham crowd in 1927

A sack race, or perhaps sack rugby?

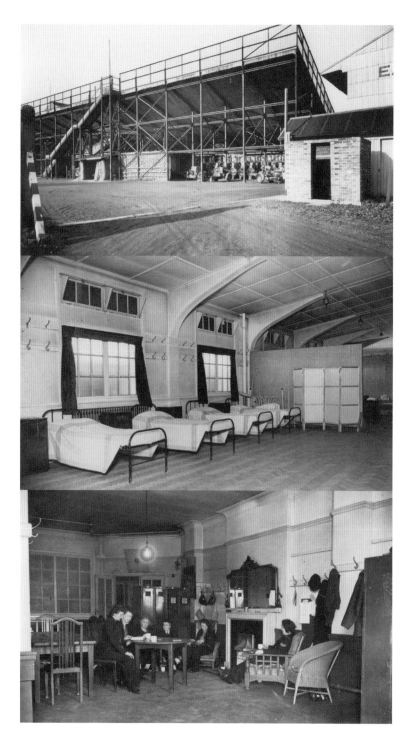

Military vehicles stored below the South Terrace

A first aid post was erected in the West Stand restaurant, in case of gas attacks

The Committee Tea Room was used as a mess area

Far right: Military ambulances lined up outside the West Stand

WORLD WAR II

THE SECOND WORLD WAR SAW THE STADIUM PLAY a far greater role in the war effort than it had during the previous conflict. Ireland's visit in February 1939 – HQ's 50th international fixture – was the last before it was requisitioned as a civil defence depot and for the next six years Twickenham was almost unrecognisable.

"Only [Secretary] Sidney Cooper and the head groundsman, Mr Hale, were left," recalled Tom Prentice, the son of former RFU President F. D. Prentice, in a letter to the World Rugby Museum. "Everyone else went off to serve in the Armed Forces. Sidney Cooper had liased closely with the Civil Defence authorities who used the place for possible decontamination processes after possible use of chemical warfare. The place was full of vehicles, the dressing rooms were stripped for installation of anti-gas equipment. The pitch itself was spared for Mr Hale to administer."

These were not the only changes at the ground. The East Car Park was cultivated for growing vegetabes as part of the 'Dig For Victory' campaign, an air raid shelter was built at the south end of the East Stand while the West Car Park was commandeered by the National Fire Service, as well as serving as a coal dump. The West Stand restaurant became a first aid post.

Twickenham was mercifully spared a direct hit by enemy bombs during the War. A V1 flying bomb did land worryingly close but it was anti-aircraft fire and a lack of basic maintenance that did the most damage and when the war ended in 1945, the stadium was looking depressingly decrepit.

"No work, repairs, maintenance (except grass cutting) or painting had been possible, so one can imagine the state the place was in as the staff, one by one, began to return in 1945 and later," observed Tom Prentice. "The roofs of the stands still had holes caused by anti-aircraft shells falling from the sky as shrapnel, the iron work was rusty, the crowd barrier weakened, woodwork and seating needing repair or replacement. The whole of the area underneath the South Terrace, which had housed Civil Defence vehicles, was infested by a plague of rats."

THE JEHOVAH'S WITNESSES

IN 1954 THE RFU EMBARKED on what was to be a long-standing relationship with the Christian 'Jehovah's Witnesses' movement, who were looking for a venue to stage a mass gathering. They offered the RFU £3,000 for the hire of Twickenham for a five-day event and, faced with a summer bereft of revenue, the Committee accepted. The convention quickly became a regular summer event in TW1 with the numbers increasing every year.

"Nearly 1,400 Jehovah's Witnesses were baptised breezily and briskly, in a 24 foot diameter pool on Twickenham Rugby Union field yesterday," reported *The Daily Express* in July 1963. "They went through the water at the rate of 15 every 15 minutes, baptized by ten 'immersers' who worked in shifts. The only difficulty came from one woman. Afraid of the water, she was in the pool nearly ten minutes before she was totally immersed as the society's beliefs require."

In 2007 more than 25,000 Jehovah's Witnesses attended the Sunday of the event and the movement and their submersion tanks remain a fixture on the Twickenham calendar to this day. A far more recent addition has been the introduction of summer concerts, temporarily transforming the home of English rugby into a huge open-air music venue.

The Jehovah's Witnesses' convention has been a regular event at Twickenham since 1954

Thousands are 'immersed'
at Twickenham every
summer

ROCKING RFU

IN THE LATE 1990s THE RFU began to give serious consideration to staging music concerts at Twickenham. South London was seriously lacking a large venue for major outdoor events, yet Twickenham lay idle for months on end outside the traditional rugby season.

It seemed a logical fit but some local residents were concerned about the impact of staging concerts in the area, noise and traffic especially. But the RFU worked hard to allay their concerns and in the summer of 1999 announced its intention to stage a concert at the stadium.

The first concert was scheduled to be an appearance by Luciano Pavarotti, backed by the Royal Philharmonic Concert Orchestra, in the summer of 1999 but the RFU failed to get the necessary entertainment licence in time and the famed Italian tenor switched his performance to Earl's Court.

"Permission for concerts to be staged at Twickenham Stadium was finally granted in October 2001 after a public inquiry," explains Fraser Cullen, the RFU's Community Relations Manager. "As part of the application process the RFU and the London Borough of Richmond upon Thames signed an agreement to set up a committee to act as a forum between the RFU, its contractors and consultants, the Metropolitan Police, local residents, the council and the local transport operators."

Twickenham finally played host to its first concert two years later as The Rolling Stones took to the stage on 23rd August 2003. Tickets for the concert had sold out within two hours of going on sale.

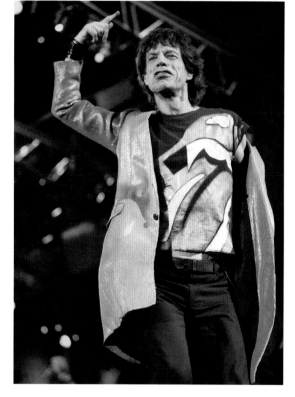

"Thundering tribal drums filled the darkening stadium, and suddenly there was Keith Richards, hammering out the unmistakable and never-bettered riff of 'Brown Sugar'," wrote Gavin Martin in his review of the gig in *The Independent*. "He was followed by Jagger, a freak of nature in a tailcoat, arms akimbo as he raced around the stage demanding total involvement from the audience.

"Jagger and an emotional Keith Richards made clear that this was almost a homecoming gig for the band, who began playing residencies in nearby Richmond back when the Prime Minister was more likely to despatch them to the Tower than to give them a knighthood."

The stadium has embraced a host of musical genres since welcoming the Rolling Stones, who returned in 2006, to the ground. U2, The Police, Rod Stewart and Genesis have all played shows at HQ and REM, The Eagles, Bon Jovi and Iron Maiden have also all dusted off their guitars for an appearance.

"The RFU retains 1,100 discounted tickets to each concert at the stadium for local residents," explains Fraser Cullen. "The planning permission allows for a capacity of 55,000 some 27,000 less than a capacity rugby match. There is a 10.30 curfew and a noise control regime for all concerts.

"The set up for a concert takes approximately six days with the huge stage constructed in front of the South Stand and the pitch covered with temporary flooring. "

Inset and far right: 'Hello Twickenham'! The Rolling Stones' Mick Jagger struts his stuff at HQ

U2 rock TW1 in 2005

RICHARD KNIGHT –
TWICKENHAM STADIUM DIRECTOR

"**T**RANSFORMING TWICKENHAM FROM A RUGBY STADIUM** to a live music venue is a big logistical challenge but we've become more experienced over the years and although capacity is 27,000 less for a concert, it is still a huge operation.

"The bands use the home and away changing rooms as dressing rooms and the Spirit of Rugby restaurant is converted into a back-of-house area for the producers and promoters.

"The biggest difference however is the use of the pitch. On match days there are 30 players and the referee on the grass and everyone else is encouraged to stay off the area. For a concert, there's suddenly 15,000 on the pitch and we have to ensure they can get in and out safely.

"We turn parts of the West Car Park into a storage area for all the production vehicles and the lorries that transport the rest of the band's equipment and depending on whether we're or not expecting a predominantly female audience, we will redesignate the toilet areas.

"The stage traditionally goes at the south end of the stadium because it provides better acoustics and also helps limit the noise dispersal from the ground. It also makes it easier to get the stage in and out plus there's better access for the trucks at that end of the stadium.

"We've had very few problems with noise since we started staging the concerts. In fact, when the Rolling Stones first played we got a call from a local man, I think he was ringing from Whitton Road, who explained he was having a barbecue and asked if we could turn the volume up."

U2 in full flow as the sun goes down on Twickenham in 2005

The Rolling Stones returned to rock the stadium in 2006

Genesis on stage at HQ in 2007

Published by Vision Sports Publishing Ltd 2010

© The Rugby Football Union. Licensed by Copyright Promotions 2010

ISBN: 978-1-905326-76-1

The Rugby Football Union

Rugby House, Twickenham Stadium

200 Whitton Road, Twickenham, TW2 7BA

www.rfu.com

Vision Sports Publishing Ltd

19-23 High Street, Kingston upon Thames

Surrey, KT1 1LL

wwww.visionsp.co.uk

Editor: Jim Drewett

Author: Iain Spragg

Designer: Neal Cobourne

Photography: Leo Wilkinson

Tries illustrations: Bob Bond

Sales and marketing: Toby Trotman

Printed in the UK by Butler Tanner & Dennis Ltd, Frome, Somerset

ACKNOWLEDGEMENTS

Vision Sports Publishing would like to thank Jane Barron at the RFU for all her hard work in getting this project off the ground, and seeing it through to the end. Particular thanks must also go to everyone at Twickenham's World Rugby Museum, especially curator Michael Rowe, Phil McGowan, Amy Rolph and also to Anna Renton who has now left for pastures new. Thanks also to Richard Prescott and Patricia Mowbray at the RFU for all their help. To Iain Spragg for his excellent words, always delivered on time, and to Leo Wilkinson for the great pictures, including the wonderful cover shot, and for going beyond the call of duty to delve around for all sorts of obscure shots. Thanks also to Terry Ward of stadium architects Ward McHugh Associates, to Claire Parnell at Nike, Paul Morgan of Rugby World and Tom Roe of CPLG Sport. A word of appreciation, too, for Geoff Nagle who kindly allowed us to publish a picture of the touch flag from the England v Wales match of 1910 which is part of his private collection.

NOTE FROM THE PUBLISHERS

In making the selections for 'Twickenham Legends', 'Great Matches' and 'Terrific Tries' we feel we should point out our selections should not be considered in any way official or definitive. As with all subjects of this nature such lists are of course a matter of opinion – we have just tried to use this book to present as many of the great players, matches and tries from Twickenham's rich history that we could fit into one book.